GREG SORBARA

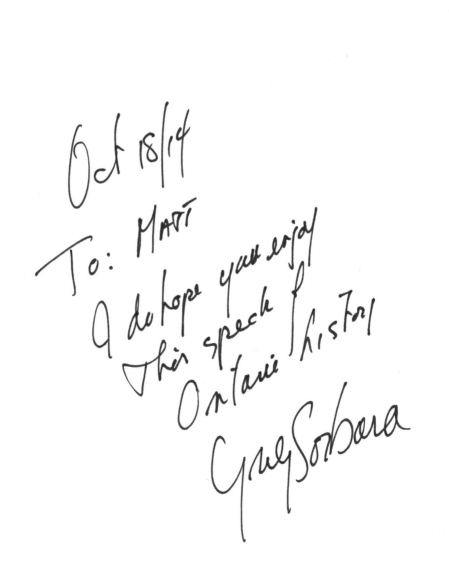

Oct 18/14

To: Matt

I do hope you enjoy
this speck of
Ontario history

Greg Sorbara

"This is a must read for anyone interested in Ontario politics. Greg Sorbara takes us on the roller-coaster ride of the past three decades encompassing seven premiers, three different parties in power, and a sea change in the province's economic and political culture. To accompany us on the ride, there is a rich supply of insider anecdotes from someone who was directly involved in all the changes."
— Ian Urquhart, former Queen's Park columnist for the *Toronto Star*, 1997–2007

"Greg Sorbara weaves the personal and political in charting the rise and fall of premiers and providing back-stories on leadership conventions, general elections, and thorny political issues. A great read for students of politics in Ontario and lots of grist for the media."
— Tony Dean, cabinet secretary and head of the OPS (2002–08), professor at the School of Public Policy & Governance at University of Toronto

"This is an immediate, informative take on twenty-five years of Ontario's political history, with a sharp eye to the future."
— William Thorsell, editor-in-chief, *The Globe and Mail*, 1989–99

"If you were alive between 1985 and 2014, you'll want to read this book — it's a winner."
— Lorna Marsden, president emeritus, York University

"An inspiring story, laced with humour and unique insight that will warm the hearts of political aficionados everywhere."
— Frank McKenna, deputy chair of TD Bank and former premier of New Brunswick

"[An] insightful book from one of modern Ontario's most influential figures. It provides deep insight and personal reflections on both the policy process and the real world of politics [and] from a man who has shaped the evolution of Ontario as much as anyone in the past three decades."
— Matthew Mendelsohn, director of the Mowat Centre at the School of Public Policy & Governance, University of Toronto

"A great story of leadership, accomplishment, and good humour …"
— Robert Nixon, former leader of the Ontario Liberal Party (1967–76)

GREG SORBARA

The Battlefield of Ontario Politics

An Autobiography

DUNDURN
TORONTO

Project Editor: Allison Hirst
Editor: Cy Strom
Design: Colleen Wormald
Cover design and image: © Ginger Sorbara
Printer: Webcom

Library and Archives Canada Cataloguing in Publication

Sorbara, Gregory, author
        Greg Sorbara : the battlefield of Ontario politics / Greg Sorbara.

Issued in print and electronic formats.
ISBN 978-1-4597-2461-7 (pbk.).--ISBN 978-1-4597-2462-4 (pdf).--
ISBN 978-1-4597-2463-1 (epub)

1. Sorbara, Gregory. 2. Politicians--Ontario--Biography.
3. Ontario--Politics and government--1985-1990. 4. Ontario--
Politics and government--1995-2003. 5. Ontario--Politics and
government--2003-. I. Title.

FC3077.1.S67A3 2014   971.3'05092   C2014-904278-7
                                                  C2014-904279-5

1   2   3   4   5   18   17   16   15   14

We acknowledge the support of the Canada Council for the Arts and the Ontario Arts Council for our publishing program. We also acknowledge the financial support of the Government of Canada through the Canada Book Fund and Livres Canada Books, and the Government of Ontario through the Ontario Book Publishing Tax Credit and the Ontario Media Development Corporation.

Care has been taken to trace the ownership of copyright material used in this book. The author and the publisher welcome any information enabling them to rectify any references or credits in subsequent editions.

J. Kirk Howard, President

The publisher is not responsible for websites or their content unless they are owned by the publisher.

Printed and bound in Canada.

Visit us at
Dundurn.com | *@dundurnpress* | *Facebook.com/dundurnpress* | *Pinterest.com/dundurnpress*

Dundurn
3 Church Street, Suite 500
Toronto, Ontario, Canada
M5E 1M2

To my dad, whose love of family, community, and
country knew no bounds

Early in my political career he sent me the letter
reprinted in Appendix 3

And to Kate
Potter, poet, painter, gardener,
and the beam of light guiding me on my way

Getting Back

We drove upstream, all the way from Montreal,
on slippery roads, beside trees burdened with ice.
I held the crossword; you the steering wheel.
Someone had given you The Beatles,
We're going Home, Two of Us, Mother Mary.

That was another time I'll tell you. We were kids,
like our kids now. The age of coupling off,
setting up house, starting a family. We were
the center of the world, knew what was important,
what to wear and where and how. We were invincible.

I looked over at you, hair graying, hunched
over the wheel, steering us over the ice, worrying
about the wipers and the rear-view mirror.
I wanted to thank you for everything.
Everything. But I didn't.

—Kate Sorbara

She wrote this in the wake of the 1998 Quebec ice storm

CONTENTS

ACKNOWLEDGEMENTS

This memoir emerged from an unrelenting desire to document a fragment of Ontario's political history from a very personal perspective. It was Robert Prichard who first urged me to consider taking the project on, and it was Bob Rae who shared the secret to actually writing such a book. He described it to me as the AOC method — Ass on Chair! I have the blisters to confirm that he was right.

First, my very special thanks go to Kirk Howard, the president and publisher at Dundurn Press, for the confidence he expressed that my story would be worthy of his printer's ink. Kirk has assembled a remarkably dedicated staff of professionals at Dundurn who share an important mission for Canadian publishing. Carrie Gleason, Dundurn's managing editor, and Allison Hirst, Dundurn's project editor, guided me through the work from start to finish. They were nothing if not patient to a fault with this apprentice author.

Over the past fifteen years, I have been blessed in my professional life with the world's best general manager, my assistant Sharon Laredo. Every aspect of this work bears her fingerprints — organizing and documenting interviews, researching the events that are retold here, fact-checking virtually every page, transcribing the scrawl that is my handwriting, consulting with those who could add perspective to the text, editing, printing, and binding version after version, and sounding the alarm as deadlines were about to arrive, not to mention managing every aspect of my relationship with Dundurn from day one. There would be no book were it not for her determination.

Many friends and former associates assisted me in the research for the book. Colin Andersen, my deputy minister while I was in finance and now the CEO of the Ontario Power Authority, reviewed chapters from that period, thus helping to remove the cobwebs that clouded some of my memories. Charles Pascal, a former deputy minister of education and a dear friend, read more than one version and in each case provided insightful advice for improving the text.

And Steve Paikin, host of TVO's *The Agenda* and the pre-eminent authority on contemporary Ontario political history, doubled from time to time as an encyclopedic and objective reference guide for some of the adventures that I have chronicled in these pages.

Cy Strom, on behalf of Dundurn, reviewed the first draft of the manuscript. His evaluation led to a thorough recasting of the manuscript. I am very grateful for that work and also for his editorial help later in the process.

Writing requires a particular discipline — one that does not come naturally to me. But it does to my wife, Kate. The example that she has set over the years working at her keyboard gave me the confidence that I could complete this new adventure.

Finally, I want to acknowledge those who believe in the importance of documenting Ontario and Canadian political history. Were it not for you there would be no purpose for this memoir.

PREFACE

The casual observer of my life can be forgiven for thinking that politics and public policy were obsessions throughout most of my adult life. Certainly, I played vigorously. From the outset, to use a baseball analogy, I tried to develop the tools necessary to stay on the major league roster. I worked on my mechanics and studied assiduously the styles of established professionals such as David Peterson, Bob Nixon, Ian Scott, Bob Rae, and, of course, Jean Chrétien. And often — too often, probably — I paid more attention than necessary to my own stats.

No doubt politics and public policy were passions for me. But my real centre of gravity has been and continues to be my family: my wife, Kate; our six children, Lucas, Carla, Ginger, Noelle, Martina, and Nicholas; and our (so far) thirteen grandchildren, Freedom, Noa, Mason, Aemon, Yael, Mira, Audrey, Alex, Sam, August, Isaiah, Esmee, and Dante.

That "team," nurtured throughout by Kate, has always been my personal wellspring. Kate's life has been a spiritual journey expressed through art and toil, at turns as a weaver, a potter, a poet, and a painter. And always with hands muddied from the soil of her glorious gardens.

For nearly forty-five years we have remained, through thick and thin, devoted to one another and to the well-being of our children and their children. Together we have learned how the power of the introvert and that of the extrovert can conspire to achieve great things, and that the rewards are far richer than what is available from a too-public life.

INTRODUCTION

The worst day of my political career — October 11, 2005 — started without any hint of the calamities that were about to unfold. I was days away from my second anniversary as Ontario's minister of finance and finally feeling a level of comfort with the work I was doing.

My first visitors of the day were Paul Beeston and Paul Garfinkel. Beeston, as he is known to his friends, was visiting as chairman of the board of CAMH, the Centre for Addiction and Mental Health. Dr. Garfinkel was the centre's president and chief executive officer. Ostensibly, the two Pauls were in my minister's office in the Frost Building, across the road from the Ontario legislature, to lobby me for more money for CAMH. But before we got down to all that, Beeston and I had to talk baseball. In 1976, Beeston was the first employee ever hired by the Toronto Blue Jays. He started out as the team's vice-president of business operations and would later go on to serve as its president and CEO. But on this day, he was visiting as a volunteer, trying to make the case for those suffering from mental health issues. Beeston was enjoying a kind of seventh-inning stretch in his life. Three years earlier, he had been president of Major League Baseball, working directly alongside Commissioner Bud Selig. Three years in the future, he would return to the Blue Jays for a second go-round as their president and CEO.

For years baseball has been a bit of an obsession for me. So having

Beeston in my office was a real treat. We had been friends since 1994 when I was the lead for a business group that purchased the Jays' minor league franchise in St. Catharines, Ontario. He's got the best belly laugh of anyone I know. We needled each other relentlessly. I told him what a fool he was for declining to give me a shot at being the team's back-up second baseman. For close to an hour, to the chagrin of the other Paul, we swapped stories about baseball *and* politics. Beeston knew his politics in part because former Ontario premier John Robarts was one of the members of the Blue Jays' original board of directors. If only all my stakeholder meetings were this much fun.

After our meeting I walked over to the legislature, where I was approached by Karen Howlett, one of the reporters in the *Globe and Mail*'s Queen's Park bureau. Karen got right to the point.

"Are you aware that the RCMP has raided the offices of The Sorbara Group as part of its investigation into Royal Group Technologies?" she asked, referring to my family's development business in York Region, run by my two brothers, and a public company on whose board I had sat.

I did not know.

"Did you know your name is mentioned in the search warrant?" Karen followed up.

I did not know that either.

The first thing that went through my mind was, *This is crazy.* "I resigned my seat on the board of Royal Group Technologies two years ago when I became minister of finance," I told Karen, "so there's no way this could involve me."

"But your name is on the search warrant," she repeated.

I was perplexed. "I am not a part of this," I persisted.

But apparently, I was.

That's how I found out that somehow I had been swept up in an RCMP criminal investigation.

I went back to my ministry office and called my political staff together. We informed the premier's office of what was going on. I called my brother Edward to see if he knew anything more. He didn't. He merely repeated what Karen Howlett had already told me.

Weeks later it became clear that my name was on the search warrant as part of an RCMP investigation into allegations of conflict of interest on the part of various Royal Group Technologies executives. But on that day I was in the dark. I tried calling the RCMP to get clarification but got no response from them. The search warrant was "sealed," I was told, so I didn't have a clue as to why their investigation involved me.

That night, around eight o'clock, I met with my chief of staff, Peter Wilkinson. Peter was a superb adviser from a great Ontario political family. He would go on to become chief of staff to Premier Dalton McGuinty. His brother John was a first-term MPP from southwestern Ontario who after the 2007 election would become a cabinet minister. Peter and I stepped out onto the balcony overlooking Queen's Park Crescent. His message was clear: "You have to resign."

I replied simply, "You're right. Let's put that in motion." And I don't mind admitting Peter and I had a good cry and a good hug in the crisp fall air. My first instinct was to fight back against what I saw was a terrible injustice. All of my efforts to get the Ontario Liberals back into power and reorganizing the province's priorities, first as party president, then as an MPP, and finally as minister of finance, had come to a screeching halt. It was surreal. But there was no fighting back that night; I had to step aside. The premier's office had to be notified, a news conference had to be organized, and a replacement as finance minister had to be selected. Since the new finance minister would no doubt be someone already in Cabinet, a new minister would have to be chosen to fill that spot as well.

I called my wife, Kate, and asked that she come down to Queen's Park as soon as possible. I wrote my letter of resignation to Premier McGuinty, then gathered the Press Gallery for a late-night news conference in the ground-floor lobby of the Frost Building.

"A rather serious mistake has been made," I told the reporters present. "But the interests of our government are greater than the interests of my personal career as finance minister." And with that, it was done. I was out.

It seemed to me that I was, in fact, announcing the end of my political career. Equal measures of confusion, anger, and shame of a kind that I have never before experienced swirled within me. In an instant I had been swept up in a criminal investigation I knew nothing about.

Somehow, I got through that news conference without breaking down. But as it ended, I remembered a quote from a journalist who, on the day Margaret Thatcher was ousted as prime minister of Great Britain, uttered the following: "Every political career ends in tears."

I thought to myself, *Maybe this is the end for me.*

On the morning of October 11, 2005, I was the second most influential person in a government responsible for spending just over $90 billion of the people's money. By that evening, I had lost something more than my Cabinet position. As a politician in trouble I had lost the public's trust. It weighed on me heavily. I had always been committed to a political life free from taint. From the outset I had wanted to show the people of Ontario that an Italian-Canadian public servant from a prominent and prosperous family could be an honest broker. Now, a baseless RCMP investigation would sow the seeds of doubt that could last a lifetime.

I feared that no matter how this misadventure turned out, every future newspaper article about me would refer to this. It would become a permanent stigma.

One thing I was determined *not* to do was crawl under a rock and disappear. On October 12, 2005, the day following my resignation, the legislature was to begin the second session of the thirty-eighth parliament with the McGuinty government's second Speech from the Throne, unveiling the priorities for the upcoming term. I showed up for the Throne Speech, clapped in all the right places, and was determined to present the image of a good team player. I don't know what my caucus-mates *really* thought, but to my face they were all supportive.

At moments such as these, some people surprise you by how quickly they disappear, while others surprise you by how unexpectedly supportive they are. One such intervention touched me deeply. A few days after my resignation, I was driving home from Queen's Park when my cell phone rang. "Greg, it's Brian Mulroney calling." I barely knew our former prime minister, but there he was on the phone, with a strong message of support. "Don't let the bastards grind you down," he said. "Fight back." For a brief moment he felt like my best friend forever.

Nearly a decade after being embroiled in an RCMP investigation that could have cost me my political career and my reputation, I can look back with a somewhat more dispassionate eye. It was, in the end, just one of the many political adventures that together lasted a quarter of a century. So it occurred to me that those adventures on the battlefield of Ontario politics might be of some value to people who are interested in public life and the human condition. It is with that purpose that I offer the stories in these pages. First, this book is *my* story. By virtue of the roles I performed in Ontario politics, I had the honour of experiencing some truly memorable things with some unforgettable people. I pass those experiences along for what they're worth. Those that also went on this journey or who observed it may, I hope, learn more about what it was all about. I worked side by side with the most successful Liberal premier of Ontario in more than a century. I also encountered some worthy adversaries, and I talk about them too. This isn't quite a "tell all" memoir, but you will learn more of the unvarnished truth than I could tell while I was still in politics. In addition, I hope this book provides some clarification for those of you who want to know how politics *really* works. I have tried in these pages to pull back the curtain and show how things get done, warts and all. You may not love how politicians accomplish some of the things they do, but after reading this, I hope you'll agree it's an honest account of one man's efforts to improve the lives of the people he served in — as Premier McGuinty used to say — "the best province in the greatest country in the world."

Greg Sorbara
Richmond Hill, Ontario
September 2014

1

From the Foot of Italy
to the Steps of Queen's Park

One of the things I've always loved about my family's background is how quintessentially Canadian it is — one of the millions of stories of immigration to welcoming Canadian soil.

Both of my parents were born in the southernmost area of Italy's mainland — the region of Calabria. My father, Sam, was born in a mountainous place called San Giorgio Morgeto in 1911. My mother, Grace (in Italian, *Grazia*), was born in the seaside town of Bovalino Marina in 1913. Together, my parents carried within them the power of the mountains and the oceans, according to my wife, Kate, who knows about these things — the two most powerful forces in nature.

Like many Italian immigrants, both of my grandfathers came alone to the new world to establish themselves before sending for the rest of the family. By the time my father came to Canada in 1925, his father had become an alcoholic and his mother was quite sick. She died within a few years of her arrival. My father, the oldest of four siblings, in effect became the presiding parent to his three siblings after my grandmother's death.

It's not an exaggeration to say that my father's family lived in real poverty in Guelph, Ontario, where other San Giorgio immigrants first settled. When the Great Depression hit, things just got worse. They did whatever they could to earn a living, including pilfering coal from the local railway yards to stay warm and bootlegging alcohol, sometimes watered down to harmlessness, for their immediate cash needs.

But the pivotal event of my father's early years in Canada came when he was arrested and sent to jail *for three years* for passing counterfeit money. I will add that my father was extremely pleased when he received an official pardon thirty years later.

Guelph was not for Sam Sorbara. After imprisonment he wanted out of that environment and hoped to become a lawyer. He somehow got together the necessary funds for tuition at St. Michael's College at the University of Toronto, where he began his education. However, within a year the registrar of St. Mike's, Father Basil Francis Sullivan, told him, "Sam, this place isn't for you. You have a family to support. Go out there, get married, and make a living." Twenty-seven years later, the then-president of St. Mike's, Father John Kelly, suggested much the same thing to me as a tactful way of informing me that I was not cutting it as a university student. It was a watershed moment in my life, as it was in my dad's.

Realizing he wasn't going to be a lawyer, Sam began selling Italian-style meats, travelling from Windsor to Montreal.

During this time my mother's father, after working for years with the Canadian National Railway and carefully saving, purchased the house next door to his own on Bellwoods Avenue in the heart of the Toronto Italian community. He converted it into a grocery store, which my mother was to run.

My parents didn't know each other in the old country. They had both left Italy as teenagers. One day, my father went into the Bellwoods Avenue store with the meat products he was selling at the time. He was twenty-nine, she was twenty-seven. If not for that chance encounter, my three siblings and I, and our parents' seventeen grandchildren and twenty-seven great-grandchildren, never would have found our way to spaceship Earth.

Later my dad went on to sell mineral feed to farmers in the Greater Toronto Area. Through the 1940s and 1950s he came to know the territory well, got serious about real estate, and started buying farms from farmers anxious to sell. Those efforts became the foundation for what would become The Sorbara Group, one of the province's long-established land development companies. It is a business that has prospered for more than sixty years, providing the necessities of life not only for my siblings and me but also for our children and now their children. It was and remains the silver spoon lodged firmly in my mouth that allowed me the indulgence of a political career spanning twenty-five years without ever a concern about the real issues of paying for rent, groceries, and the like.

Once my parents married, they started having kids right away: Joseph in 1942, Edward in 1943, Marcella in 1944, and me, the youngest, in 1946. Until I was born, the family had been crammed into small living quarters in the back of a newer, larger grocery store at the north end of Bathurst Street.

Eventually my father started making a good living selling insurance and real estate. Just after the Second World War and before I was born, he built a new home on the edge of the city of Toronto just south of where Highway 401 was to be built.

There wasn't much overtly Italian about our family — or our neighbourhood for that matter. Most of the kids at my school were Irish-Catholic. Peter O'Rourke was my best friend. My parents only occasionally spoke Italian in the home, and then only to each other, when they wanted to keep us out of the conversation. English was our official language. And yet an abiding pride of heritage remained. By the mid-1950s my dad was emerging as one of the leaders of the growing Italian-Canadian community in Toronto, often one of the "founding fathers" of Italian-based organizations like the Canadian Italian Businessmen's Association (now known as the Canadian Italian Business and Professional Association). Countless new arrivals would come to see him for advice on getting established in the new country. After the wounds of war with Italy healed, he and two friends intervened with their personal resources to repatriate Casa d'Italia — the consulate of Italy in the heart of Toronto confiscated by Canada during the war — on behalf of the Italian government. It remains the Italian consulate today.

Because language is essential to culture, my dad insisted that all of us learn to speak Italian. My tutoring started at the age of twelve, when I trekked down to the University of Toronto for private Italian lessons every Saturday morning. When I was fifteen, my dad, along with Joseph D. Carrier Sr. and his son Joe Jr., took me to Italy for a summer to study Italian with a private tutor. There was no way of knowing then how important his determination about language would prove to be for me and the political career I would embark upon twenty-five years later.

In my first campaign, cast as an upstart Italian Canadian challenging a well-established Tory incumbent, I was able to build a much more intimate relationship than he with the burgeoning new Italian-speaking population in my riding. We simply spoke to one another in the mother tongue.

Through the 1950s and in the early 1960s Italian immigrants were coming to Canada in massive numbers. Compared to that wave, the Sorbaras were part of a small but influential Italian-Canadian population in the Toronto area. As kids we were deeply rooted in Canadian soil, felt no part of an "ethnic minority," and were determined to compete with our peers no matter what their origin.

For me, competition took place primarily in the classroom and in the parish church, St. Margaret's Catholic Church, a few doors away from our home, where I became an altar boy of some renown. The good Sisters of Loretta expedited my passage through grade school so that by my twelfth birthday I was enrolling in high school at St. Michael's College School under the tutelage of the Basilian Fathers. St. Mike's was hockey and religion with a vengeance; I bought the whole package. By age sixteen, in grade 12, I saw my vocation — to become a Basilian priest following in the footsteps of my high school hero Father David Bauer.

After high school graduation I became a novice in the Basilian novitiate in rural Mississauga. The novitiate year is one of monastic meditation and prayer prior to admittance to the seminary. But the calling did not endure: I lasted three months. To be brutally honest, although not yet sexually active, I missed the company of women. I realized that the cloistered life alongside an all-male cast of clerics in robes was not for me.

In a bit of a daze I enrolled in the University of Toronto and quickly learned to skip classes, avoid exams, and smoke marijuana. After four sporadic years, with one year of credit, and with Father Kelly on my case, I packed it in. Concerned counsellors suggested that social work rather than business might be the right path for me.

While none of them suggested I prepare for the life of a future Ontario finance minister, I knew even then that public issues held far more allure than did private ones. Indeed, I thought that preaching politics might be a somewhat better fit than preaching redemption.

Every single person who becomes an elected official gets there in his or her own unique way. There is no road map. I'd been fascinated by politics since I was a young kid. I was thirteen years old when I watched John F. Kennedy speak at the Democratic National Convention that picked him as the party's standard-bearer in the 1960 election against Richard Nixon. I was enthralled by the hoopla of the political convention.

In 1962, I was part of a Young Liberal expedition to Ottawa where we met and were addressed by Lester B. Pearson, then the Leader of the Official Opposition and soon to be prime minister. I was captivated by Pearson, lisp and all, and by the grandeur of the parliament in which he worked.

In 1967, Canada's centennial year, I joined the Company of Young Canadians for a two-year stint as a volunteer. It was a path suggested to me by one of the counsellors who assisted with my abrupt departure from university. The CYC was an ambitious and daring organization launched by the Pearson government with architecture similar to President Kennedy's Peace Corps. I was assigned to work with young dropouts in the heart of Vancouver.

In the Company my colleagues were young radicals bent on changing the world. My group started a free school for at-risk teenagers determined to tune in, turn on, and drop out. The school was called Knowplace. We were young revolutionaries, and whether by nature or nurture I soon became the political spokesperson for our "revolutionary cell."

In the spring of 1968, drugs were everywhere, and I found myself at a gathering in the home of a friend of a fellow CYC volunteer. Our host had a capacity for recreational drugs that I had never witnessed before or since.

Late that afternoon two other CYC volunteers arrived at the party — Lynn Curtis and the woman with whom he was living, Kate Barlow. He was a Vancouverite and she was the daughter of a dairy farmer from Aurora, Ontario. She was working at another free school in North Vancouver.

There is no other way of putting this — it was love at first sight. Indeed, by the time I headed back that day to my quaint bedsitting room in Kitsilano, I was certain that I would spend the rest of my life with Lynn Curtis's live-in girlfriend, Kate Barlow, even if there was no indication that she felt the same way about me.

We were doing the same kind of work and shared the same circle of friends, mostly associated with the CYC and the free school movement. Within months I heard that she and Lynn were planning to marry and settle somewhere in rural British Columbia. I was not deterred. It would only be a matter of time, I decided. And it was.

By the spring of 1969, Kate had been hired on a short-term contract to care for an eleven-year-old severely autistic girl named Margo Coleman, while the authorities searched for a permanent foster home for the child. And Kate's relationship with Lynn was coming to an end.

The summer of 1969 was truly the summer of love. Kate and her friend Judy Pruss had set up camp, with Margo in tow, on one of the most remote beaches on Vancouver Island, a sandy stretch at the bottom of Radar Hill close to the fishing village of Tofino. I was a frequent visitor and soon a permanent guest.

By the fall, Kate and Judy and Margo had moved to a suburban house in Chilliwack in the Fraser Valley, an hour from Vancouver. I travelled back and forth in a badly beat-up Volkswagen. By February Kate was pregnant. I was in heaven.

Truth be told, Kate and I were polar opposites. I was an extrovert on steroids, a city boy on a mission. She was an introvert with a healthy distaste for society's mundane tastes. For her, matters of the spirit, solitude, reflection, and creative energy were what really counted. And she was an artist. Over our forty-five years together she has been a weaver, a potter, a poet, and a pianist, and most recently a painter, all to inspiring effect. In every one of our years together, wherever we were, she would grow a grand summer garden.

By August 1970, Margo was permanently in our care, and we were headed back to Ontario so I could join the staff at The Everdale Place, another free school in the village of Hillsborough, a stone's throw from Guelph.

Lucas was born two months later. So unprepared were we that his first cradle was the drawer of an old dresser in the farmhouse that we had rented near the school.

Over that winter we concluded that we were not yet ready to be Ontarians again and decided in June to return west, this time to the Slocan Valley in the West Kootenay Mountains of British Columbia, where so many of our Vancouver friends were retreating to go back to the land.

For the summer we lived in a teepee on the banks of the Slocan River. It was magical.

By September we had found and purchased our first real home, an unfinished 20-by-30 A-frame house that included six acres of hillside. By winter we had a cozy home, no electricity or phone, cold running water, a wood stove, and a potbelly heater. Down the path was the outhouse. It was a pastoral idyll that soon included a milk cow, some chickens, and a mangy farm dog.

Carla arrived in February 1973 and Ginger in November 1974. By then, we had built a large addition that included all the creature comforts that electricity and indoor plumbing could provide.

Kate often reminds me that we were never happier in our lives than we were during those years "in the valley." And while that was true, the extrovert in me grew increasingly restless. I needed the kind of social engagement that Kate was just as happy without. I devised a plan to get a law degree and return to the valley as a small-town lawyer, and I pleaded with her to buy in. Against her better judgment, she did.

In August 1976 we returned to Ontario, to a family-owned farm in Maple. I was about to start school, and Kate was about to enter the third trimester of her fourth pregnancy. Noelle was born on December 5. Two weeks later, a fire in the farmhouse nearly consumed us all. We were lucky to be alive, but it was all still very hard on Kate. Often I would return from school to find her in tears, inconsolable. Leaving the mountains was a jolt to both of us.

Still, the demands on us would continue to grow. I completed my bachelor of arts degree at Glendon College in May 1978, and we promptly returned to the valley for the summer. By September, back in Toronto, I was finally a law student at Osgoode Hall Law School. In November the twins, Nicholas and Martina, were born. We now had six of our own and Margo, and my first set of law exams were two weeks away.

The plan had always been that we would return to our mountain home after law school. I imagined the life of a small-town lawyer with a generous amount of time for political activism: a legal education would give me the tools I would need to do both. Indeed, six years earlier, in 1972, I had become fascinated with the notion of running for the federal NDP nomination in our rural B.C. riding. My admiration for Lester

Pearson notwithstanding, my time in the Company of Young Canadians could allow for no other partisan choice. Besides, by 1972, Trudeaumania had soured through much of Canada, and certainly in rural and small-town British Columbia.

Mercifully and gently, Kate helped me overcome my delusions of grandeur. She reminded me that I was only twenty-six years old and not quite ready for prime time.

During my second year at Osgoode Hall, to my surprise I was invited to article at the relatively new Toronto office of the well-known Montreal law firm Stikeman Elliott. The notion of returning to the mountains, to the valley, and to the lifestyle that we had known there was placed on permanent hold. In the interests of my career, we had suddenly became fully repatriated Ontarians.

My ongoing interest in politics really began to blossom in June 1984, when I somehow talked my way into being a delegate at the Liberal leadership convention in Ottawa. I recall wandering around the Ottawa Civic Centre, filled with awe and wonder at the notion that I would be helping select the next prime minister of Canada. Pierre Trudeau had stepped down after his famous walk in the snow four months earlier, and the smart money suggested the convention would come down to a choice between John Turner and his rival, Jean Chrétien, with whom I cast my lot.

Turner won on the second ballot to become Canada's seventeenth prime minister. As for me, my initiation into the world of politics had begun.

Five months later, in November 1984, I was courted by the Ontario Liberals to be a candidate in the following year's provincial election. My recent involvement in Liberal Party politics and my family's well-known last name in York Region probably led Vaughan Councillor Nick DiGiovanni and Liberal Party worker Loretta Serafini to my doorstep.

The possibility of one day being a member of parliament had been in the back of my mind for years by this time, but always as a member of the federal parliament in Ottawa. I had considered myself a "Lester Pearson Liberal."

Strangely, it was now the provincial Liberals who were knocking at my door. Before deciding to run, I thought it appropriate to find out more about the man who was leader of the party.

I didn't know David Peterson at all, but I wanted to see whether I could feel comfortable running for him. I called the Leader of the Opposition's office at Queen's Park to set up a meeting. The voice answering the phone said, "Pat Sorbara speaking."

"Who the hell are you?" I asked.

"Who the hell are *you*?" she shot back.

Despite the fact that we were directly related (Pat is the daughter of a cousin of my dad's), I had never met her. But this was a wonderful way to meet. It felt like an omen. Pat was at that time a key political staffer for David Peterson. Three decades later she was back at Queen's Park as Kathleen Wynne's campaign director for the 2014 general election. Many pundits credit her with playing a significant part in the surprising victory that gave Premier Wynne a new majority mandate on June 12, 2014. It was our party's fourth election victory in a row.

David Peterson and I met for an hour, spending most of our time talking about our kids. I got a very good vibe from him, and I left thinking this was a guy I could travel with. In February 1985 I decided I had to give it a try.

Frankly, the prospects were not great. The riding of York North was about as safe a Conservative seat as existed anywhere in Ontario. But privately I thought things just might turn out differently. There was a tectonic shift happening in Ontario politics, and I could sense it. Lots of people could. The forty-two-year dynasty of the Progressive Conservative Party felt shaky. Bill Davis's departure as one of the province's great premiers changed the political and social dynamic. The Tories had a tried, tested, and true formula for renewal that had proved successful since 1943. When it came time to change leaders, they would choose someone with moderate credentials from the next generation of leadership. That stopped in January 1985 when the party selected Industry and Trade Minister Frank Miller from Muskoka, an unabashed right-winger several years older than Davis. It felt to me as if our leader, David Peterson, was a more logical inheritor of the Davis mantle than Miller. Peterson was a pragmatic centrist, forty-one years old — the same age as Davis when he became premier in 1971 — and not an ideological conservative like Miller. Furthermore, I've always believed that Ontarians like to hedge their bets. If they put one party in power federally, there's a stronger likelihood that they'll put a different party in power provincially. In September 1984, voters had given Brian Mulroney's Progressive Conservatives more seats than any party in Canadian history. I thought that might also help give the Ontario Liberals an opening. Finally, in my own riding, the Tory member, Bill Hodgson, was seventy-two years old and failing in most of his capacities. He had an increasingly difficult problem with alcohol and came from the white, Anglo-Saxon, underpopulated north part of the riding. Conversely, the population growth was in the mostly Italian community of Woodbridge, with which I had a cultural relationship. I thought I could speak to the new, more modern York Region in a way Hodgson couldn't. I thought I had a shot at winning.

In the midst of the campaign, my friend and mentor, Dennis Mills, asked me a question that surprised me greatly: "Why do you want this job, and what do you hope to achieve if you get it?"

I was taken aback. Why indeed did I want to become an elected member of a provincial government? Since leaving the novitiate I had been drawn to political causes: fighting to modernize the Catholic Church, marching against the Vietnam War, advocating for street kids in Vancouver, and finally abandoning the world of commerce for the lifestyle of the "back-to-the-landers."

Back at school at thirty, I immersed myself in Canada's history and its political history in particular. Laurier, Pearson, and Trudeau became heroes. At law school I tried to come to grips with the structure of Canadian lawmaking and the ironies of Canada's constitutional makeup.

The answer to Dennis's question only slowly started to emerge. I came to realize that everything I had done for fifteen years and more was an apprenticeship for a role in a Canadian legislature. Despite the radical days of the sixties I was decidedly a liberal and content to be a Liberal politician. While I was not well schooled in provincial matters, I relished the opportunity to represent a riding at Queen's Park. A clearer opinion on myriad provincial issues — education, health care, social services, human rights, and sexier issues like beer and wine in the corner store (or not) — would come in time. I came to answer Dennis's question by speaking about my hope to bring a more liberal approach to the public life of Ontario's citizenry. During the campaign I began to speak about electing a more inclusive, more transparent government, and electing a parliament that reflected the real face of the province. That included a stronger voice for Italian Canadians and voters from the various cultures that represented the future of the province and the country.

The election campaign of 1985 was simply a wonderful experience. The PC campaign made mistake after mistake. Frank Miller declined to participate in a leaders' debate, which brought him an avalanche of unflattering publicity. And our guy Peterson ran like someone without a care in the world. He was out there having fun, pitching truly progressive policies.

I had only one significant encounter with Peterson during the campaign. It was in the Aurora Arena about a week before election day. Dennis Mills hired Ronnie Hawkins to rock the joint, and he did. I had a little chat with Peterson on his campaign bus, and then watched him wow the crowd as Ronnie, David, and I sang "Bo Diddley." It made newscasts across Ontario.

Election day was May 2, 1985. On that day, my Aurora campaign manager Steve Budaci told me: "You've run a great campaign. But you're probably going to lose by five thousand votes." I retorted: "That's just great, but I've been going door to door for five weeks and you're full of shit. I'm going to win."

The verdict in York North: perhaps Bill Hodgson should have retired, perhaps it's time to give someone else a chance, maybe this David Peterson guy is okay. I won the seat by 4,100 votes. I was going to become a member of the Ontario legislature.

I was a politician.

2

The Peterson Years

The result of the 1985 election was virtually a tie. The Progressive Conservatives captured more seats than we did (fifty-two to forty-eight), but we got more of the popular vote (38 percent to 37 percent). The NDP, under its new leader Bob Rae, won twenty-five seats and thus held the balance of power in parliament.

Almost immediately speculation arose as to whether Frank Miller's minority government could survive. The winds of change were sweeping Queen's Park. Discussions between the Peterson Liberals and the Rae New Democrats began within hours after the election; within days an accord was signed under which the NDP agreed to give parliamentary support to a Peterson-led Liberal government for a period of two years. The accord also set out a number of policy issues that were to be pursued during those two years.

The change of government was now only a matter of time. Miller presented a Throne Speech on June 4, 1985. Fourteen days later his government was defeated on a motion of no confidence supported by the two opposition parties. David Peterson was to become premier. During that short-lived Miller parliament many memorable speeches were made as we debated the motion to end forty-two years of Tory rule. The best came from parliamentary legend Robert Nixon. Nixon's dad, Harry, had been the last Liberal premier of Ontario in 1943, before the Tory dynasty began.

Bob Nixon had already been an MPP for twenty-three years, all of them in opposition. And yet, for a man who would finally get a taste of government after all those years, he was admirably gracious in his remarks.

"Forty-two years of Conservative rule, not all of it bad, is coming to an end," he said. "We'll have a peaceful transition. No one will be shot. No riots in the streets. It's a tribute to democracy." I felt that this speech nicely contrasted with outgoing premier Frank Miller's speech, which sadly was far too angry and bitter.

As for me, I was a thirty-nine-year-old rookie who was simply shocked at how quickly I had gone from nominated candidate, to election night success, to potential minister in David Peterson's government.

Ten days before the election, my campaign manager in York North told me, "You know, David Peterson just might win this election, in which case you should start lobbying now to be in the new Liberal Cabinet."

It was the first time such a possibility had ever occurred to me, and frankly, it filled me with dread, given my lack of political experience. I pushed back, telling him, "Let's take this one step at a time, okay?" I wasn't entirely superstitious, but it seemed a bad omen to start promoting a personal agenda so far in advance of having the actual election results behind us.

Once the realities of the election and the accord were clear, I had more and more people approach me, saying, "David Peterson really should put you in Cabinet." No one said exactly why, but I inferred that I was a bit of a new face, that I had campaigned well, had an Italian-Canadian background, and was from York Region. That checked off a number of criteria Premier Peterson would want to see represented in his new Cabinet.

Contemplating the possibility of being appointed to Cabinet was both enlivening and disconcerting. For the first time I realized that very soon I might take on a role that would give me star status within the Italian-Canadian community. I would be the first so-called Italian-Canadian to serve in an Ontario Cabinet. It would be something that I would have to manage delicately. So many others, including my dad and my brothers, had worked for years to strengthen the fibre of the community. I, on the other hand, had no record of participation. In no small measure I felt like an outsider in a community that would soon be required to celebrate my achievement.

Under the circumstances, I remained anxious about the possibility of being appointed. I had spent no time at Queen's Park, didn't know how the process worked, and had no previous political experience to point to. I determined that it would be best to make no contact with the incoming premier's staff, nor did I want to know whether others were going to bat for me behind the scenes.

Thus, the day before our new Liberal government was to be sworn in on June 26, 1985, I waited in our caucus room at Queen's Park, along with all the other members of the Liberal caucus. One by one we were summoned into Peterson's office to receive our marching orders. I thought I'd be told I was about to become a parliamentary assistant. That didn't happen. It was a very quick meeting.

"Greg," the premier-designate said, "I want you to be my new minister for colleges and universities, and minister of skills development." Not one but *two* portfolios.

"I'm honoured and will do the best I can," I said to Peterson. He advised me to make it my business to get to know every college and university president in the province as quickly as possible. But he also said something that perplexed me. "I know there's some stuff in your family background, but we're not going to worry about that."

Stuff? What did he mean by that? Did he mean my father's imprisonment? Did he mean a letter I'd sent to the RCMP in a fit of pique many years earlier, urging them to stop arresting people just for smoking dope? I didn't ask for clarification, but I did wonder.

One other thought occurred to me. It was just four short years ago that I'd graduated from a university with a law degree. Now I was to be responsible for the entire post-secondary system.

Crazy.

Almost immediately after my meeting with Peterson, I did something rather unusual for me. Despite my altar boy past, I hadn't spent a lot of time in churches over the past quarter century. But at that moment I needed a quiet sanctuary to think about what had just transpired. I needed a place to calm myself. So I went to a sanctuary I knew well, St. Basil's Church at St. Michael's College, a short walk from Queen's Park, and prayed for inspiration.

June 26, 1985, was a spectacularly beautiful day. We held the Cabinet swearing-in ceremony on the front lawn at the south side of Queen's Park. Thousands of people came to the afternoon ceremony to see the first Liberal government in forty-two years sworn into office. As my turn came, my doubts started to fade. I took the gorgeousness of the day as an omen and thought, *I can do this.* My anxiety began to vanish, and I started to ponder what we could accomplish.

This was one of the smallest administrations ever, with only forty-eight Liberal MPPs. I was one of nine rookies sworn into Cabinet. The caucus and Cabinet coalesced quickly into a tight-knit unit, determined to stick together and make things happen. Solidarity was the order of the day.

Strangely enough, the first Cabinet meeting was mostly memorable because of an unexpected person who showed up. Apparently, a woman watching the swearing-in ceremony took Premier Peterson's invitation to experience a "government without walls or barriers" very seriously. We were several minutes into our first Cabinet meeting when people noticed a woman in the room whom nobody seemed to know. There were a lot of rookies around that table, and the civil servants didn't know us all. Eventually we discovered she was a member of the public who figured it was okay to sit in on this new, open government's Cabinet meetings! Alas, we disabused her of the notion that our government was going to be *that* open, and she was escorted out.

After assuming the responsibilities of my new portfolios, one of the first things I had to do was assemble my support staff. The key appointment in any minister's office is the chief of staff, or what back then we called the minister's "executive assistant." Oftentimes, the premier's office will appoint executive assistants for new ministers, but I had someone in mind for the post and David Peterson's office went along with my choice.

I wanted an old law school friend of mine named John Morrison. John was a neighbour of Bob Rae's in the west end Toronto neighbourhood of Baby Point. He had worked like crazy to help me get elected in that first campaign. Sadly, things just didn't work out with John, and within a matter of months people were advising me to terminate him. It wasn't John's fault. He knew me, but he didn't know politics all that well, and as a result I had to let him go. It was a heartbreaking moment in our relationship. It destroyed a friendship with John and his wife Andrea that was the strongest Kate and I had developed since we returned to Ontario from the west. And it was the first of many events that reminded me that the harsh realities of politics so often trump things that enrich the lives of private citizens.

Barbara Sulzenko, who had a wealth of experience working at the federal level for former deputy prime minister Herb Gray, took over. Barbara's depth of insight into public policy and partisan management was just what this political rookie needed to make a positive mark during the Peterson years.

For the most part, the first Peterson administration was all sunshine and light. There was a real sense across Ontario that there had been a sea change in the politics of the province. David Peterson was quickly becoming the country's most popular — and most debonair — political leader. Needless to say, eventually we wanted to turn our small minority government into a majority. But we were still fairly green and thought that by working hard we'd be rewarded by the electorate when it came time to go back to the people. Liberals hadn't been in power for forty-two years. We were simply focused on getting things done.

And we did. Ontarians experienced one of the most activist governments in their province's history. We led the inaugural session of the new parliament with the introduction of Ontario's first ever Freedom of Information Act, a clear display of how we wanted to govern "without walls or barriers." We embarked on social housing projects as never before; we were environmental activists, particularly with the worst polluters in the province. We passed the "Spills Bill," which sent a shiver through the boardrooms of large industries. It was good law and policy. We banned the practice of doctors extra-billing their patients beyond what the health insurance plan's fee schedule allowed. We put television into the legislature. There was pay equity, pension reform, and much more — including the blue box recycling program, which became a signature for Jim Bradley in his first term as Ontario's environment minister.

Part of our success in those first two years came from the strength of our front bench — perhaps the best in Ontario history. As premier, David Peterson was in his glory — popular across the province and in love with the job. As treasurer, Robert Nixon was the master of the legislature, disarming opponents with his sense of humour. Nixon understood how Ontario's system of government and its legislature worked in a way that no other player could. He had been part of the place since his childhood. Ian Scott, as attorney general, could never be outdone in a question period duel. And Education Minister Sean Conway, first elected to the legislature at age twenty-four and now responsible for implementing one of our key (and most controversial) promises, extending full public funding to the Roman Catholic school system, was unassailable. We were happy to be in government, loyal to one another, and displayed a caucus solidarity that I don't think has ever been replicated.

Even when we got in trouble, the winds at our back were favourable. Our only northern MPP, René Fontaine, was made minister of northern affairs and mines. René was a wonderful guy, but not particularly attuned to the nuances of conflict of interest. So even though he was the mines minister, he traded some of his mining stock, a clear no-no. But he came up with a neat way to cleanse the blemish. He quit not only the Cabinet, but also his job as MPP. "You want to accuse me? I'll quit and run again," he said.

I went to Hearst in northern Ontario to speak at René's nomination meeting. For some reason, he took a bit of a shine to me; I suspect it was because he saw us both as activist Liberal businessmen, despite my lack of real business experience. We had good chemistry. It was at this nomination meeting, for the only time in my life, I spoke entirely in French. To be honest, I'm not entirely sure what I said or if I said it well. But he got nominated, won his seat again, and was back in Cabinet. The sad postscript to René's story is that his tenure in public life probably cost him $1 million or more and the demise of his businesses. The sawmills which were the source of his wealth began to fail as the downturn in forest products grew; his businesses required his energy and oversight to keep them afloat. But he was in Cabinet and could not be engaged in any way in private business affairs, including his own.

Elinor Caplan also got into some trouble and resigned from Cabinet for a time. That experience led us to create the province's first conflict of interest legislation and to appoint a conflict of interest commissioner. Other provinces later followed suit. It was, I believe, the country's first major effort at modern transparency in government.

As the minister of skills development, I had the responsibility to implement one of the most ambitious promises of the Liberal campaign — a guarantee of two years of employment for all disadvantaged young people in Ontario. I began to learn how a minister's political staff works with the civil service to move policy forward. Barbara expertly understood the system of policy making, including how to work with my deputy minister, a young protégé named Blair Tully. I could measure our government's acceptance by the civil service according to the way Tully described us. At first, we were "your government." Then he called us "the government." But before long we were "our government." (It was one of my saddest duties to give a eulogy at Blair's funeral, when he succumbed to cancer in 1999 at age fifty-three. I was extremely touched that his wife asked me to speak, despite our not having worked directly together for almost a decade.)

The collaboration between my staff and the civil service worked like magic and resulted in "Futures," a program directed exclusively at disadvantaged youth. It turned out to be a tremendous success. It changed the lives of hundreds of thousands of young people whose employment prospects had been very dim indeed. Three things contributed to making Futures such a success. First, of course, was the political commitment led by Peterson to dedicate hundreds of millions of dollars to improving the prospects of disadvantaged young people. Second was the program design that emerged from a very talented ministry of skills development staff. And third was the fact that the Ontario economy had started to grow again, increasing governmental revenues and enhancing overall demand for young workers.

The ministry of colleges and universities kept me busy, as did skills development. First up was the cleanup required by a long and divisive strike in the community college system. Part of that cleanup involved changing the structure of the board of each college to provide for representation from both the faculty and staff. Most college presidents thought that Armageddon had arrived. We persevered, and once the changes were implemented most boards provided demonstrably better governance.

Because the economy was growing again we had resources to increase grants to both parts of the post-secondary system and to embark on a large number of infrastructure projects. The one that made me happiest was a new building for Algoma University College. Although the building was small in size, it sent a clear signal to Sault Ste. Marie that there would be no more talk about closing down this tiny jewel of a university. Our mission was to help it grow.

Premier Peterson kept his word and completed the two-year mandate agreed to in the accord with the NDP. Shortly afterward, however, he asked the Lieutenant-Governor to dissolve parliament. Our polling looked extremely favourable. There was widespread acknowledgement that we had done our level best to implement the items agreed to in the accord, and now was the time for the public to render its verdict on Peterson's minority government.

In fact, the numbers suggested we could win a clear majority. The premier's popularity was never higher. The Tories under Larry Grossman were in disarray. With some justification, the NDP may have thought it was entitled to a generous share of the credit for the policies set out in the accord, but the public preferred to give the credit to us.

David Peterson called the election for September 10, 1987. Campaigning would be a summertime affair, filled with images of the premier enjoying himself at endless backyard events. We calculated that as long as we could run a mistake-free campaign, we'd come back with a majority. One of my competitors in York Region must have thought the same thing. Don Cousens, the Conservative who represented the riding of Markham, said to me, "Greg, I'll stay out of your way, you stay out of mine, and we'll both get to return to Queen's Park." I was okay with that. Don was as strong a constituency representative as any in the legislature. He eventually went on to be the mayor of Markham from 1994 to 2006.

I'll confess, I had a bit of a soft spot for Larry Grossman, and not just because he too was an incurable baseball fan. He took over a PC Party that was sinking. He was up against the most charismatic politician in the country in Peterson. But while Larry was a very effective cabinet minister in Bill Davis's government, he just couldn't compete on the charisma scale with our guy.

Election night 1987 was a shell shock. We simply did not imagine such an overwhelming victory. Ontario Liberals won 95 out of 130 seats in a newly enlarged legislature. There was much to celebrate, and no one thought this result had an iota of downside. We had almost fifty new members, all of whom were thrilled to be at Queen's Park. Yet there was one odd comment in our first caucus meeting after the election. Premier Peterson told us, "I got you elected this time. But next time, you'll have to get me elected." It seemed an unusually dour thing to say amidst all the euphoria. It also turned out to have been incredibly prophetic.

Within days of the election Peterson set to work designing his new Cabinet. I took the same approach as before: no lobbying. However, a few days before the new Cabinet was to be sworn in, I got a call from my legislative assistant Bob Richardson.

"The word is, you're going to Labour," he told me.

As far as I was concerned, that was awful news. During the two accord years, the only Liberal cabinet minister constantly under attack was Bill Wrye, our minister of labour from Windsor. The NDP saw labour as its special constituency and so it put Bill through hell. I phoned Vince Borg, the premier's executive assistant.

"What in the world did I do to offend your boss?" I asked aggressively. "Why am I being sent to Labour?"

Vince tried to placate me. "It's going to be okay, Greg. We've got something else for you as well."

The "something else" turned out to be a second portfolio, minister responsible for women's issues. In fact, I'd be the last male to hold that portfolio.

By the time David Peterson called me to offer the new double-barreled portfolio, I had calmed down. In fact, I was looking forward to what I could do in the job. In our first term we had promised to bring in pay equity as part of the accord with the NDP. It was now left to me to implement it within the labour ministry.

While I loved my previous portfolios, the reality was they didn't often require me to be up on my feet in the legislature to answer questions. With labour and women's issues, that would all change. And I did wonder whether I could withstand the attacks from the other side. Within a short time I began to find my voice in parliament and to fall in love with my new responsibilities. I worked on Workers' Compensation Board reform with its fine chairman, Robert Elgie, the former Tory labour minister. The board was on its way to insolvency and it was my responsibility to bring a better regime to pensions and benefits. It put me squarely in the crosshairs of NDP leader Bob Rae and his labour critic Bob Mackenzie. The workers' compensation reforms resulted in the most violent protest at the legislature in years, as the Union of Injured Workers stormed the building, blew past security, and marched right up to the stained glass doors of the legislative chamber. The NDP, in my view, truly misrepresented what we were trying to do, but they had decided this was their battleground and they wanted a big fight over it. Ironically, it took Bob Rae's leaving question period and coming into the lobby outside the chamber to pacify the protestors.

I may have been at war with organized labour on the workers' compensation issue, but I worked closely and harmoniously with Ontario workers to improve health and safety in the workplace. I developed a respect for labour leaders such as Bob White of the Canadian Auto Workers union, Leo Gerard of the United Steelworkers, and Gord Wilson of the Ontario Federation of Labour. I wanted to get two things done: first, to allow employees to legally refuse to work in unsafe workplaces, and second, to create a requirement that every workplace have a health and safety committee and safety training for its workers. So we introduced a bill providing for those two things. The day one coverage was very favourable. The media described it as historic, dramatic legislation. Colleagues were patting me on the back for bringing it forward.

And then all hell broke loose.

The major corporate interests in Ontario — the Canadian Federation of Independent Business, the Ontario Chamber of Commerce, and others — raised bloody hell with the premier. At almost every Cabinet meeting thereafter, Premier Peterson would make some off-hand remark about the "goddamned health and safety legislation."

But my health and safety bill was not the only thing that was challenging for the government, and the mood of Ontarians was turning demonstrably against us. Several things conspired to make this new, much bigger government more challenging. Unlike the first caucus, which was small and busy, our class of '87 was huge and, for too many members, not challenging enough.

While our first year went well enough, by 1988 we began to be overtaken by national issues. The Free Trade Agreement (FTA) between Prime Minister Brian Mulroney and U.S. president Ronald Reagan initiated a divisive national debate that was only resolved by Mulroney's second election victory in 1988. It caused an enormous dilemma for Peterson, who felt the need to call the agreement into question, against the wishes of so many of his business and corporate friends who'd supported him and the agreement. On reflection, our cautions were not justified. The FTA has been beneficial for both countries.

But there was more. Peterson became increasingly engaged in the national unity file, convinced that the very viability of the country was at stake unless the Meech Lake Constitutional Accord could be passed. At the time, the first ministers of the country saw what they thought was an opening to get Quebec's signature on the Constitution, something that had eluded Pierre Trudeau when he and nine of the premiers repatriated the Constitution with an accompanying Charter of Rights and Freedoms on April 17, 1982. Of course, Trudeau had a separatist premier in René Lévesque to deal with, making a deal with Quebec all but impossible. Brian Mulroney, conversely, had Liberal Premier Robert Bourassa as a potential partner this time, giving the pro-Meech forces hope that a deal could be consummated. Once the first ministers came to an agreement at the Langevin Block in Ottawa in 1987, every legislature in the country had three years to ratify the deal before it could take effect. Ratification ultimately failed in both Manitoba and Newfoundland.

My problem was that I was against Meech Lake. I thought Trudeau had it right, that the agreement surrendered far too much federal power to the provinces, and gave Quebec extra undefined powers through the famous "Distinct Society" clause. Apparently, word got out among Peterson's staff that I wasn't onside with the agreement and was considering voting against it. I had now been in politics for three years and was starting to develop my own political views. I agonized over whether my job as an MPP was to vote my conscience, represent my constituents' views (whatever that meant), or toe the party line. On June 28, 1988, as government members gathered in the East Lobby before the vote, David Peterson pulled me aside. "You are part of the Cabinet and you're voting for this," he told me. It wasn't a threat. But it was a clear direction. It was one of the few occasions during my time in politics that I felt significantly compromised. The only response I could muster was to say, "I understand that, Premier." And I voted yes.

I noted with some consternation that Chaviva Hosek, another cabinet minister who opposed the agreement, was permitted to skip the vote. In Chaviva's former life she was head of the National Action Committee on the Status of Women. Women's groups were opposed to Meech Lake and, for some reason, Chaviva was given a pass for the day. I wasn't so lucky.

Ontario became the sixth province to ratify the Meech Lake Accord. This was yet another lesson in my ongoing political education — how to live with and through a collective decision to which I, as an individual member, was quite opposed. Indeed I wondered then and later whether my hope of voting against Meech Lake was in part driven by the notion of grandstanding to the praise of those in the country who agreed with Pierre Trudeau's opposition to the accord. It also taught me an important lesson about the dynamic tension that is an essential ingredient in the collective decision-making process that is part and parcel of our parliamentary system. Still, I was not unhappy when Clyde Wells in Newfoundland and Elijah Harper in Manitoba closed the file on the Meech Lake Accord. Harper, the first Aboriginal member of the Manitoba legislature, blocked passage of a ratification vote in Manitoba by declining to give his consent to a motion to proceed with approval without public hearings. (Such a motion required unanimous consent of all members.) In Newfoundland, Wells, who was an outspoken critic of Meech Lake, declined to put a ratification motion before his legislature, citing the futility of doing so given ratification's impending failure in Manitoba.

Adding to our agonies was, of course, the Starr Affair which was now starting to dominate headlines. Patti Starr ran the Toronto chapter of a century-old organization called the National Council of Jewish Women. She loved being the centre of attention and loved the notoriety that came from raising money for our party. The only problem was that it was illegal for charities to raise funds for and donate money to political parties. Even worse from our standpoint was that one of our best campaign backroom advisers, Gordon Ashworth, got ensnared in the scandal when he and his wife accepted a refrigerator from donors associated with Starr. In time, Premier Peterson called a public inquiry on issues relating to Patti Starr. That put the affair on the back burner during question period but ensured endless bad headlines for us as the inquiry heard increasingly inflammatory allegations about the Liberal Party's relationship with Starr.

But there was more. Peterson sold his family business to York Region businessman Marco Muzzo for $10 million. Three million dollars of that ended up in the premier's blind trust. The sale was completely defensible, but it added to the odour of scandal. Finally, there was the growing

THE PETERSON YEARS · 43

perception that David Peterson was becoming preoccupied with national issues at the expense of the more mundane matters within the exclusive purview of the province.

The solution devised by the premier's office was to chart a new course by way of a major Cabinet shuffle. It was August 2, 1989, and it came to be known as the night of the long knives. Several ministers, including Chaviva Hosek, were dismissed, and others shuffled. I was somewhat more fortunate.

I was simply demoted.

I had come to love my association with labour and women's issues. We had dealt with violence against women, expansion of women's shelters, implementation of pay equity, and settlement of a difficult strike at de Havilland. The issues were politically challenging and invigorating. Coming off a successful run at colleges and universities, and skills development, I had the temerity to believe I was heading in the right direction politically as well.

I've seen numerous ministers try to explain away or put the best face on demotions over the years. It's hard to do because everyone realizes you really aren't thrilled to be leaving work you loved for work you're ambivalent about. In the political pecking order, you go from being a major leaguer to a Triple A player. But apparently, Peterson needed to send a message to business that the guy who caused so much grief at Labour was getting knocked down a peg.

I was sent to consumer and commercial relations, where I would have political responsibility for alcohol, church-basement bingo, and the Cemeteries Act: in other words, far from the contentious issues of the day. But there was one item the ministry was studying that had the potential for big headlines and big headaches: casino gambling in Ontario. I told officials there that I knew casino gambling would inevitably become legal in Ontario. But I did not want to be the minister to bring it forward. It was not something that I wanted in my political CV. Three years later it was left to Bob Rae and his NDP government to actually legalize casinos in Ontario, a rather shocking *volte face* for that party.

As it turned out, I wouldn't have much time to fret about changing the policies of this ministry. One year after the shuffle and just three years into a five-year mandate, David Peterson decided to call another election.

It would turn out to be not such a good idea for Liberals.

Unlike the 1987 election call, which was essentially the decision of the premier's office, this one was different, as we headed toward the last days of the 1980s. The subject of election timing — go now or go later — was often discussed in caucus and Cabinet. The majority of caucus wanted no part of an early election. The premier seemed genuinely open about the issue. But the strategists saw a recession on the horizon. They also saw a new PC Party leader in Mike Harris, selected in April 1990, who seemed far too right wing to be a serious challenge. And, of course, the NDP had never won an election in Ontario history and didn't feel like a credible threat this time around. The conventional wisdom was that we'd lose some seats but win a fresh mandate if Peterson called an election before the recession kicked in.

I was skeptical. I didn't like the look of things.

Maybe an election might present Peterson with an opportunity to re-engage with Mr. and Mrs. Ontario. The premier loved to campaign, and he was great on the hustings. Perhaps calling an election would give him a new sense of energy for the next mission. But for me, the timing just wasn't right.

In June 1990 at a Cabinet meeting, I summoned up the courage to say what was on my mind. "Premier, some people out there don't feel good about our party right now," I began. "And some people don't feel good about you." I had to put it out there, knowing it wouldn't make me more popular with the boss. But it was true.

At our final Cabinet meeting in late July, we went around the table one last time. "I understand this ship is well out of the harbour," I said referring to the election call I knew was coming. "But I've just gotta say, I think we're making a terrible mistake. We may win re-election, but we'll lose a lot of good members." Only Jim Bradley agreed. Everyone else at the Cabinet table seemed to think, *The election's on, let's just get it over with and get back to business.*

No one at that table allowed for the possibility of a defeat.

In hindsight, we should have seen it coming from day one, when an environmental protestor named Gord Perks (now a member of Toronto City Council) sabotaged the premier's campaign kickoff by crashing his opening statement. Shortly after Peterson began to describe why the election was being called, Perks went to the podium, upstaged the premier, then proceeded to recite a manifesto of failures on the part of the Peterson Liberals, particularly on environmental issues. It was offensive. It was wrong. And it sent a chill through all of us.

Day by day the campaign ran into trouble, and no one could figure out how to put it back together again. Late in the campaign the premier offered a one-point cut in the retail sales tax. Rather than jump for joy at the prospect of a tax cut, people were offended by the notion that they were being bribed with their own money.

A week before election day I got a call at home from our treasurer, Robert Nixon. He had spent almost a quarter century in opposition, waiting for his chance to get into government. Finally, in 1985, he had made it. Now he was contacting me with disquieting news.

"I'm just calling to see how much you like going to matinee movies," he said, "because that's what you get to do when you're in opposition."

Since I wasn't privy to any of our internal polling, I really wasn't sure how bad things were until Nixon's call. A week earlier, I was in Thunder Bay, campaigning with Lyn McLeod. When I returned to my riding and resumed campaigning in Woodbridge, one voter set me straight. With a thick Italian accent he said, "Mr. Sorbara, I'm going to vote for you. But everyone else on my street is voting NDP."

I immediately told my campaign manager, "From now on, this campaign isn't about the Ontario Liberal Party or David Peterson, it's about one question only: who can do the best job of representing the newly created riding of York Centre at Queen's Park."

If we were going to hold the seat, we needed to make local politics the ballot question. As much as people had fallen in love with David Peterson in 1987, they had apparently fallen out of love with him by 1990.

Conversely, Bob Rae was having a marvellous campaign. He was light, funny, combative, and reckless in his criticism of Peterson and the Liberal government. He did not have a care in the world. Rae had no expectation at the outset of winning the campaign.

To this day I am convinced that the voters were not particularly eager to elect an NDP government. But they did want to send David Peterson a message. Unfortunately, that message contained a political bomb. Peterson lost the election and his own seat. Bob Rae, who a few weeks earlier had contemplated quitting politics after what he assumed would be another loss, instead became Ontario's twenty-first premier. The NDP won seventy-four seats with just 37.6 percent of the vote — an incredibly efficient result. We lost fifty-nine seats. After forty-two years in opposition and just five years in power, we Liberals were headed back for another long stint in the political wilderness.

3

The 1992 Leadership

The first time I seriously considered the possibility of becoming the leader of the Ontario Liberal Party was on election night 1990. While Liberals were going down in flames all over Ontario, I hung on to York Centre by a sizeable 9,200-vote margin. As a hundred or so of my supporters gathered at La Riviera banquet hall to celebrate and commiserate, my speech to our volunteers was interrupted by chants of "Leader, Leader, Leader!" It was at that moment I realized I might need to confront the question of running to lead our party. And, perhaps naively, I liked my chances.

But my priority that night was elsewhere. The fact was, we still had a leader named David Peterson, even though he had lost the election and gone down to personal defeat in his London Centre riding. He was still the leader and I thought we all needed to respect that.

In the ensuing weeks I did very little to evaluate the leadership question other than personal fretting. Peterson quickly fell on his sword and stepped down as leader, and Robert Nixon, as the "senior statesman" in caucus, assumed the interim leadership. (It was actually the *fourth* occasion on which Nixon would lead the party — twice by winning a convention, and twice on an interim basis.)

But Nixon stepped down in the summer of 1991, accepting an appointment from Premier Bob Rae to become the Agent General of Ontario in the United Kingdom. And so, our caucus chose Huron-Bruce MPP Murray

Elston to take up the interim leadership, on the understanding that he not seek the permanent position. Elston was a solid cabinet minister from 1985 to 1990. He was the minister of health who brought in the ban on extra billing — without a doubt one of the most high-profile and controversial issues with which we dealt in our first two "accord" years. Even with the clock ticking on an eventual leadership convention, I still wasn't feeling any urgency to deal with the issue.

There were plenty of good reasons *not* to seek the leadership. I had first been elected only five years earlier. I didn't know the party well. I had never participated in a leadership campaign before at any level, other than to show up at the June 1984 federal Liberal convention and vote for Jean Chrétien. I didn't understand the delegate-selection process well or a lot of the other behind-the-scenes mechanics of running a convention. Moreover, I was hardly a rising star in the party, having been demoted in the last Cabinet shuffle. I had spent my political career trying to be a hotshot minister at the expense of visiting riding associations and getting to know the party. And, of course, a leadership bid would put a heavy burden on Kate and our six children.

To be sure, I always thought I'd run for my party's leadership some day. I just wasn't sure this would be the right time. I may have been a stranger in a strange land at the 1984 convention, but I found the experience fascinating, exhilarating and worthy of more exploration. I would also be the first so-called ethnic candidate ever to seek the Ontario Liberal leadership in an increasingly multicultural province. I was a good communicator. I also thought being elected for the first time in 1985 was a bit of an advantage. I was neither an "old-timer" in the party nor someone from the class of the '87 landslide. Of course, lots of people came up to me and told me that I ought to be a candidate for the leadership. But I didn't take those comments terribly seriously. The fact was, very few of those people were fellow caucus-mates. Only Alvin Curling and Ed Fulton, both from Scarborough ridings, and Kingston's Ken Keyes were early supporters. There was certainly no groundswell, no "Draft Sorbara" movement. If this were going to happen, it would require a lot more ambition on my part and a lot more support from within the party, and I wasn't sure I had it.

But by September 1991, with the convention still five months away, I began to get more interested. I struggled with how I would share this news with my wife. Kate had carried so much of the family workload during my five years in the Peterson Cabinet. She also knew how demanding a leadership campaign would be. Still she stuck by me right through to the last moments of the convention.

The first task was to get a campaign manager signed on. I approached Gordon Ashworth, a guy with loads of experience in politics. He took a pass, suggesting that in the wake of the Starr affair he might be more of a liability than an asset. Others suggested political organizer (and future senator) Isobel Finnerty, and so she signed on as my campaign manager along with Allan Golombek, who had been a speech writer for David Peterson.

Even though I was a novice with little sense of how demanding a leadership run would be, I initially found myself — as strange as it sounds — in the thick of the competition, with a decent shot to win. My primary competitor was Lyn McLeod who succeeded me as minister of colleges and universities. Her two main operatives in the campaign were my former legislative assistant Bob Richardson and my cousin Pat Sorbara.

For those Liberals who were seeking the opposite of what we'd had as leader, McLeod was their candidate. David Peterson was now seen as an urban, slick, out-of-touch male who'd been in politics for almost twenty years. McLeod was a northern, rural, down-to-earth, caring woman with barely four years of provincial experience behind her. She was the "un-Peterson."

The other candidates were fellow caucus-mates: Charles Beer, the MPP for York North; Steve Mahoney, the MPP for Mississauga West; and David Ramsay, the MPP for Timiskaming. Given the field of candidates, I liked my chances of being on the last ballot. Beer was a solid, serious guy, but lacked the royal jelly necessary to win. Mahoney had decent support from some quarters, but often seemed more vaudeville than premier-like. Ramsay seemed to be running to solidify his Liberal credentials, having first been elected in 1985 as a New Democrat.

In 1985, Vince Kerrio and I were the first Italian Canadians in Ontario history to be appointed to the Cabinet. It was a good indication of how Ontario was changing. But as I campaigned for the leadership, I got frequent reminders of how much of Ontario still *hadn't* changed. In Metro Toronto my Italian heritage was not an issue. But on the Bruce Peninsula, or in eastern Ontario, I felt a coolness that I attributed to my background. I saw references in the media to my being "the ethnic candidate." I had never seen myself that way, but apparently others did. From my first days as a candidate in 1985 I had avoided fashioning myself as an "Italian-Canadian" politician. As a practical matter I considered my parents' cultural origins as but one more element in my makeup and one that added richness to my life and a special ability to connect with large and vibrant Italian-Canadian communities across Ontario. However, this leadership campaign was only a year and a half removed from the Patti Starr scandal, where the names of Italian land developers were nefariously tossed around in the media. I just got the sense that when people looked at my candidacy, they thought, "This guy's Italian, the son of a land developer, and he wants to lead our party? I don't think so."

But then a bombshell hit the leadership race. In November 1991, Murray Elston announced he was going back on his commitment *not* to be a candidate. He resigned the interim leadership, jumped into the race, and became the immediate front-runner. My reaction when I heard the news: "That son of a bitch." It felt like a betrayal.

In fairness, Elston was under inordinate pressure to go back on his word and enter the race because many Liberals weren't satisfied with the field of candidates. He had been a strong cabinet minister and member of caucus, and there was no official prohibition preventing him from getting in, other than that he'd given his word.

Elston's flip-flop changed the dynamic of the race entirely. Suddenly I felt the wind go out of my campaign's sails. While I still expended enormous energy calling and meeting as many potential delegates to the convention as possible, I now understood that I wasn't going to win, that it was now an Elston–McLeod contest. Still, I wasn't going to let that prevent me from giving it my all, enjoying the experience, and getting to know my party and my province much better.

In hindsight, it's amazing how similar on policy issues all of the campaigns were. My friend and former chief of staff, Barbara Sulzenko, with a big assist from her husband, Nate Laurie, grabbed the reins of the policy development process and led the way in putting my platform together. I wanted the accent on economic development with an eye to full employment for the province. Frankly, all of us wanted to continue the agenda we were pursuing during the Peterson years and, in the process, hammer Bob Rae for his poor economic record.

I left all the fundraising for my brother Edward to organize. Edward is an admitted political chameleon. Whenever he's asked which party he supports, his answer is always, "Whichever one is in power."

Running for the leadership was beyond a full-time job. You're just constantly on the phone, travelling, debating your competitors, doing interviews, doing media training, and, of course, occasionally showing up at Queen's Park to attend question period. Just as the best hitters in baseball spend hours and hours taking batting practice to get better, the best politicians do hours and hours of media training for the same reason. Everyone thought I needed help becoming a better speaker, so I worked at it like crazy.

We made "Ontario: It's Worth Fighting For" our campaign slogan, and I incorporated it into all of my speeches. If I were in Sault Ste. Marie, I'd tell the people that the Soo was "worth fighting for."

Some leadership campaigns become bruising, personal, vicious affairs. This wasn't one of them. It was collegial, with little acrimony, even after Elston got in. Steve Mahoney and I developed a wonderful rapport, particularly when it became apparent neither of us was going to win. We often travelled together and ate meals together before debates. I didn't do it with a view to getting his support as the inevitable end of his campaign drew near. I just enjoyed his company.

As we approached the convention weekend, I knew I'd be coming third on the first ballot, but I never once allowed myself to think about whom I might throw my support to on subsequent ballots. I'm sure members of my campaign team were meeting with their opposite numbers on other campaigns about subsequent ballot support. But I never did. I simply focused on what would be required to move from third to first, recognizing that at that point in history, it had only happened once before. (Joe Clark won the 1976 PC leadership, coming from third place on the first ballot.) Stéphane Dion won the 2006 Liberal leadership doing the same. Dalton McGuinty came from *fourth* place on the first ballot to win the 1996 Ontario Liberal leadership race. But those other examples hadn't happened yet. My possible victory from third place in 1992 was an unlikely long shot.

I guess the best evidence that led me to believe we weren't going to win came in the days following Christmas 1991. For the previous ten years, Kate and I had been putting our kids in a van and driving to Florida for a two-week vacation. Now we were just five weeks away from the leadership convention and every minute counted. Nevertheless, I said to my campaign team, "Sorry about this, but I'm going to Florida, and we'll pick up from where we left off when I get back in January." They were extremely unhappy with me, but in this case I couldn't let my political agenda get in the way of my family agenda. That time together was too precious.

My first taste of any leadership convention came in 1960, when I watched the television coverage of John F. Kennedy's bid for the Democratic presidential nomination. I saw him give his speech and was riveted by the drama. It may be hard to believe, but I said to myself, some day I want to do that too. Now that day had arrived. It was February 8, 1992, at Copps Coliseum in Hamilton, the hockey arena named after Sheila Copps's father, Victor, who was once the mayor of Hamilton. (And his middle name was Kennedy!) I was totally in the moment, taking in all the hoopla and thinking about how to outdo my competitors during the speeches before the vote.

Convention speeches generally come together when the candidate's speech writer produces a first draft, meets with the candidate, goes over whatever improvements the candidate wants, and then massages the speech a bit more until everyone's satisfied with it. We tried it that way on my campaign, too. But that just didn't work for me. Allan Golombek wrote something but I simply didn't feel comfortable with it. Allan and I got into a huge brouhaha after I told him I just wanted to go to the podium, not with a word-for-word text to read but rather point-form notes I could talk from. I knew that tradition suggested that just wasn't done, but talking extemporaneously was a method that had always worked for me. I felt I could be my most authentic self by talking to the delegates rather than reading something someone else had written.

So right up until it was my turn to go on stage, I stayed in my hotel room and scribbled down ten pages of handwritten point-form notes. I knew if I just let the ideas flow there would be more passion and mission in the address.

I wanted to start with a line from David Peterson's 1990 election night concession speech, when he said with great dignity: "There is no disgrace in getting knocked down; there is only disgrace in not getting up again." I continued: "This party is back on its feet again, and we are going to win the next election!"

I knew any chance I'd have to win required a Hail Mary pass, a speech so good it would make undecided delegates give my candidacy a second look. Luckily the speech went so well that even Allan Golombek came up to me afterward and said so. Writing in the *Toronto Star* the next day, columnist Thomas Walkom said it was the "best over-all speech" of the night.

Perhaps it was an indication of my own political naïveté, but I really thought a great speech could change the outcome of the next day's first ballot. It didn't. Murray Elston came first with 740 votes, or 30 percent of the delegate support. Lyn McLeod was second, nipping at his heels with 667 votes, or 27 percent support. As expected, I came third, but with 345 votes (14 percent) I was too far back to represent a credible alternative. Beer, Mahoney, and Ramsay pulled up the rear. From that moment on, everyone in the hall knew it would come down to either Elston or McLeod.

The conventional wisdom among second-tier candidates today is that you only have the power to influence the outcome if you move quickly to another candidate. Back in 1992 it didn't work that way. Campaigns had worked hard and wanted to stay on the ballot as long as possible. Whereas today the bottom *three* candidates might have left the race right after that first ballot in hopes of influencing the outcome, on that day in 1992 only Ramsay departed after the first ballot, and he endorsed no one. I was hopeful Charles Beer might drop off and endorse me. But when he didn't, I admit I was a little heartbroken. I was one of the people responsible for Charles's successful campaign in 1987. Before that election, I had called him and urged him to run for the party again, even though he'd already run and lost in two previous elections. I paved the way for him to run in the new York North riding, carved out from the much larger riding I had represented from 1985 to 1987. I liked him. But neither Charles nor Steve Mahoney was open to my campaign's pleas to join us.

There would be five candidates on the second ballot. Murray Elston picked up 27 more delegates for a total of 767, but Lyn McLeod grew the most and showed the convention some semblance of momentum. Perhaps because she, like Ramsay, was from the north, she added 77 delegates to her count. My campaign tally grew as well, adding 35 delegates for 380 in total. But that still only represented 16 percent of the total, leaving me still in a weak, rather than threatening, third place. As the last-place finisher on the second ballot, Steve Mahoney would have to drop off.

Again, it was decision time for those pulling up the rear. From the time the results were announced, candidates would have fifteen minutes to indicate whether to stay on for another vote or move to another candidate. I spent those crucial fifteen minutes trying to buck up my troops, while giving the campaign team the space they needed to solicit support from the other candidates. But there was none to be had. Mahoney, no doubt sensing the biggest wave of momentum was with McLeod, supported her. Beer would stay on for another ballot, a disappointing turn of events for my campaign.

On the third ballot, the convention got truly exciting. The momentum Lyn McLeod enjoyed on the second ballot continued for the third, as she passed Elston and moved into the lead. But it was a razor-thin margin. McLeod captured 873 votes, good for 35.9 percent of the delegates. Elston took 865 votes for 35.6 percent support. I continued to pick up some more support, and now had 402 votes, or 16.6 percent. Beer's decision to stay on for another ballot was ill advised: he lost 18 votes for a total of 289, falling to only 12 percent support. He would have to drop off for the fourth ballot vote. I still remember my sense of profound disappointment when he moved to Lyn McLeod's section of the arena. In hindsight, I guess the numbers spoke louder than the personal friendship I thought we had. But I was crushed.

The fourth ballot continued to excite the crowd. McLeod extended her lead over Elston, 1,049 to 988 by votes, or 44 percent to 41.5 percent. It looked as if it were in the bag for her. My staying on to fight the fourth ballot was rooted more in hubris than in any realistic chance of winning. This five-month odyssey would soon be over, and I wanted our team to experience it right to the bitter end. I simply didn't want the game to end yet. More important, I was having a terrible time determining what my next move should be.

With only 341 votes, representing 14 percent of the delegates, I now had to drop off. I met with representatives from both the McLeod and Elston campaigns. I was truly torn. In my heart, my head, and my gut, I just didn't think McLeod had what would be needed to rebuild the party and get us back into the winner's circle. As for Elston, I could not get over his late entry into the race.

What came next was possibly the most memorable speech I had delivered over six years in politics. It was certainly the most emotional. I gathered my delegates as close together as I could, and with megaphone in hand I told them how grateful I was to them for sharing this journey with me. I told them it was now their turn to make the next move: "Think about whom you want as your next leader and support that person. That's democracy." I told them I wouldn't be endorsing anyone.

Some people later said it was a cop-out that I didn't play kingmaker or queenmaker at that convention. And there may be some wisdom in that. But I just couldn't do it. I lined up to cast my fifth and final vote of the convention, took the ballot, and dropped it *unmarked* into the box. I couldn't reward Elston for going back on his word, but I didn't want to reward McLeod with a sense of confidence she had not earned in my view.

The political drama reached a crescendo when the results were announced. I actually felt very happy for Lyn and was hoping to be proven wrong about her abilities. And, in spite of everything, I felt bad for Murray. The final count was shockingly close: McLeod 1,162, Elston 1,153. Nine votes, less than half a percentage point, separated the two candidates. Incredible.

The instant the results were announced, I felt all the ambition and interest in politics ooze out of me, as if someone were letting the air out of a balloon.

Later that night Kate and I were in our suite at the Sheraton Centre near the arena, just the two of us. Some late-night Liberal revellers knocked on our door asking, "Is this where the party is happening?" I replied, "No, we're from out of town. The party's happening somewhere else." And off they went as Kate and I smiled at each other.

There was one additional oddity about the final ballot results. There were a surprisingly high twenty-one spoiled ballots on which the delegates had written in my name despite the fact I wasn't eligible to be on the ballot. These were people who evidently confronted the same conundrum as I had and simply couldn't vote for either of the candidates on the fifth ballot. The next morning, when Kate and I drove home, we arrived to the sight of twenty-one pink flamingoes on our front lawn. It was as touching a moment as any I had experienced during the campaign. And a fitting end to the adventure.

In hindsight, despite ultimately not being a serious contender in the race, I had no regrets. My relationships with the other candidates quickly returned to normal. There were never any conversations with Elston about his going back on his word, or with Beer about not supporting me. There was just no point.

How long does it take to get over a leadership race defeat? Well, how long does it take to get over losing the love of your life? Politics is a very jealous lover. For most people, running for a party leadership is a once in a lifetime thing. You just don't get over it quickly.

For several months I pined about what I might have done differently. Should I have gone on the attack against Murray? Should I have been more critical of Lyn? Was I simply too personally ambivalent about whether I really wanted to win? Did I simply fail to inspire the party about my ability to return us to the government benches? Was the party simply not ready for a wealthy middle-aged Canadian of Italian heritage who had an unbridled passion for politics? Probably.

One thing was for sure. It was not long after the convention that I decided I would not run again. This is not uniformly the case in the leadership battles, but it is also not uncommon. Having set my sights on the top job, I felt a growing lack of interest in any lesser assignment. Add to that my personal doubts about a Liberal victory in the next general election, and the die was cast.

Moreover, when I saw the challenges our new leader faced in rebuilding the party after our 1990 defeat, a big part of me began to feel happy that I hadn't won. The task was enormous. I think Murray Elston felt the same way. He resigned as an MPP on Halloween 1994 and returned to his young family on the Bruce Peninsula.

The first decision I had to make was whether to leave right away or complete my term in the thirty-fifth parliament. I saw no reason to leave early. I'd made the commitment to my electors to serve out the term, and so I resolved to do so. But the reality was that I was accustomed to working the eighty hours a week that cabinet ministers work. In addition, as the Bob Rae government sank deeper and deeper in the polls, the premier decided after the Christmas break in 1994 not to bring the House back at all in 1995. So instead of echoing the sounds of the regular parliamentary sitting from February to June in the final year of Rae's mandate, the legislature was effectively shut down. As a result, my MPP's role had become a part-time job. I used the opportunity to explore other things I could do, preparing for a new life out of politics.

A fascination with post-Soviet Europe led me to the development of some business ventures in the Czech Republic, each of which led to new insights into the history and beauty of Central Europe, and led, as well, to far too much travel and very little profit.

And then there were adventures in baseball. It was a time when Canadians were engaged in a passionate, new love affair with America's favourite pastime. The Toronto Blue Jays were back-to-back World Series champions in 1992 and 1993; across the country, kids, including my son Nicholas, were storming community baseball leagues for their turn at bat.

I wanted to get in the game as an owner and developer. To that end, I financed a plan to build a state-of-the-art Florida-style baseball complex in suburban Toronto. The key component of this "Ontario Baseball Centre" would be a minor league franchise that would play its home games in the pretty-as-can-be four-thousand-seat stadium with real grass and real grit.

With the help of Senator Keith Davey, I assembled a group of twenty enthusiasts to purchase the minor league Blue Jays single-A affiliate in St. Catharines, one of fourteen teams playing in the New York–Penn League. Some of the St. Catharines–based owners — notably advertising guru Terry O'Malley — wanted to keep the team in the Garden City. Others supported my dream of eventually moving the team to Brampton.

Alas, neither plan worked out. I was unable to raise the capital to build the stadium, and our game attendance in St. Catharines was usually anemic. But for five years, twenty baseball enthusiasts could maintain cocktail party bragging rights about their ownership of a baseball team. Not quite George Steinbrenner, but at least in the same business.

The party ended when we sold our franchise to the New York Mets. They promptly relocated the franchise to a gorgeous, publicly funded new stadium in Brooklyn, New York. I suppose we could have taken some small credit for bringing baseball back to Brooklyn. Mostly, I was left with a scar of sadness that I was yet one more Canadian entrepreneur who had sold out to more powerful American interests.

In a very real sense, baseball was therapy for me. It helped me make the transition from one sport that I had loved — politics — to another that required a very different set of skills.

By June 1995, when Bob Rae dissolved Parliament and called an election, the transition was complete and my political career was fading to black.

Or so I thought.

My parents' wedding day. Grace and Sam Sorbara, June 28, 1941, Toronto, Ontario.

The Sorbara siblings: (left to right) Edward, Joseph, Marcella, and me, at the dedication of the Sam and Grace Sorbara Wing at Villa Colombo, 2004.

With Jean Chrétien at a campaign fundraiser, 1985.

With David Peterson on the campaign trail, 1990.

The 1992 leadership convention, Copps Coliseum, Hamilton, Ontario.

Blue Jays' fantasy camp, Dunedin, Florida, 1999.

With my wife Kate at an Ontario Liberal Party fundraiser, 2002.

Reading to the children at a public school in Maple, Ontario, 2004.

4

Back with a Vengeance

June 3, 1999, was Dalton McGuinty's first election as Ontario Liberal leader. He was up against Premier Mike Harris, who was contesting his third election as Progressive Conservative Party leader — a clear advantage for the governing PCs. No rookie leader had won an election in Ontario since 1971, and McGuinty certainly didn't look as if he was going to break that streak. The Tories' television ads portrayed the Liberal leader as "just not up to the job," and the fact was, compared to the veteran Harris, he wasn't. But in the dying days of the campaign it became apparent that if you were an Ontario voter and you wanted to stop Mike Harris from winning a second consecutive majority, you really had only one option: Dalton McGuinty's Liberals. The New Democratic Party under Howard Hampton was just too far behind in the polls to stop Harris, and the antipathy for the premier was so intense that even traditional NDP voters left the party to vote Liberal in hopes of preventing Harris's re-election.

It didn't work. Harris won again. However, the other story of the 1999 election was that McGuinty finished a strong second, actually getting a higher percentage of the total votes cast than Frank Miller in 1985 or Bob Rae in 1990 — and they both won. So yes, 1999 represented a loss. But I felt it also represented a solid foundation on which to build.

Two months after that election, I got a call from the Leader of the

Opposition. "I'd like you to consider running for president of the party," Dalton asked me.

This was not part of any life plan I was considering at that time. I had been out of office since declining to run for re-election in 1995, and was enjoying doing things that had nothing to do with politics. However, I considered myself a loyal Liberal and took the view that when the leader calls and wants something you have to take the request seriously. I met with Tim Murphy, the outgoing president whose future would include being chief of staff to Prime Minister Paul Martin. (Most recently, Tim co-chaired the successful 2014 Ontario Liberal general election campaign.) I told Tim I'd be open to doing the job as long as I didn't have to run for it. The last thing I wanted was to jump back into electioneering and find myself hip-deep in an acrimonious fight for a volunteer job. Tim's response didn't fill me with confidence. He thought an uncontested race *could* be done, but I could tell he was fudging.

The fact was there were forces in the Ontario Liberal Party that were coalescing around an anti-McGuinty candidate for president. And that candidate was my former Cabinet colleague in David Peterson's government, Alvin Curling. Curling himself didn't seem so determined to dump Dalton. But plenty of people around him were.

I made it clear that I would not be interested in the presidency if I had to campaign for it. But two things helped change my mind. First, I felt strongly that if the party got into a cycle of electing a leader, losing an election, and then dumping the leader, it would be a long time before we got back into power. Second, I didn't think Dalton had been that bad in the 1999 campaign. Admittedly, I was in the minority, but I thought he did pretty well. Beyond that, I thought he could win next time out.

So I changed my mind. I'd been an MPP for ten years and had no desire to do that again. But I was about to turn fifty-four years old and enter a phase of life where, if you have the means to volunteer for something you care about — in this case helping out in the backrooms — then you should.

Back in the day, campaigns for these kinds of volunteer positions were quite genteel. We decided those days were gone. So I assembled a sharp group of party stalwarts, some of whom had been with me for years — Tony Genco, Jim Evans, Steven Del Duca, and Sharon Laredo — who put together as aggressive a campaign for president as Ontario Liberals had ever seen.

My first campaign stop was at a riding association meeting in Toronto's Etobicoke–Lakeshore. Our 1999 election candidate, Laurel Broten, and her team were there. I gave my first speech on why I wanted to be president and the changes I wanted to make. In an instant I realized I enjoyed being back in the game. From the get-go, the support for my candidacy was abundant. I got to know the real mechanics of how the party functioned, beginning with the people who stuff the envelopes. I learned how riding associations really work. In the process, I developed a real affection for our troops on the ground, the unsung heroes of any political party.

The vote would take place at the party's annual general meeting, at which delegates were asked to weigh in on two big issues. First, did they want to confirm McGuinty as leader? Second, did they want Sorbara or Curling as president? It was a thrilling, leadership-convention-like atmosphere at the Ottawa Convention Centre in which the province's Liberals overwhelmingly confirmed they wanted to stay the course with McGuinty as their leader and wanted me as their president.

One thing I knew at this early stage of the game — I had no intention of treating the presidency as an honorific appointment. We had one mission and one mission only: to win the next election. To do so we would need a far more aggressive approach throughout the organization. My first step was to get the talented Sharon Laredo onside. "You got me this job, now you've gotta help me do it," I told her. She had previously worked for Liberal MP Paddy Torsney in Ottawa, but now she would assist me in all things presidential.

Given that the Dalton McGuinty who ran in 1999 wasn't yet the same guy who would win three consecutive elections, I did run into some skepticism after taking the job. I was routinely admonished for my assertion that we Liberals were going to win the next election and that Dalton McGuinty would be the next premier of Ontario. "Just watch us," I said boldly, paraphrasing Pierre Trudeau.

What does the president of a political party do? I would come to learn the answer to that question: almost everything and anything. It's the president's responsibility, along with the executive council and the political staff in the leader's office, to recruit candidates, raise money, help develop policy, create a province-wide organization, and develop a communications plan — all of the behind-the-scenes plumbing that becomes the foundation for the leader to succeed in the general election.

One of the first things I did was extremely controversial at the time: I fired the man who years later helped make Barack Obama president! Several months after the 1999 election, the Liberal Party of Ontario contracted with Chicago-based election guru David Axelrod to work with Dalton McGuinty. Axelrod was both affable and super-smart. Once a month the party would pay for our leader to travel to Chicago, where Axelrod would put him through his paces and try to develop a more confident style.

I was dead set against the arrangement. Our party wasn't sufficiently flush with cash to afford it. Moreover, I was afraid of stories surfacing in the media that in a province of almost thirteen million people our party couldn't find a single political consultant who could improve our leader's fortunes, and that we'd had to go to the United States for this kind of training. Finally, I didn't think an American political consultant could understand the nuances and traditions of the parliamentary democratic system. So I told the folks in the Opposition leader's office that our campaign director, Don Guy, and I would take a trip to Chicago to meet with Axelrod. He was completely gracious as I explained our concerns and my doubt as to whether we would continue the arrangement. He liked Dalton and wished him success. Years later, when Barack Obama won his election for president in 2008 with plenty of help from Axelrod, I thought this is the same fellow whose contract I had to cancel almost a decade earlier.

The next thing I wanted to attack was the process for nominating our candidates. Too often in the past I'd heard horror stories about how unfair our process was. For example, to become the party's official candidate one would have to sign up as many new members as possible and ensure they showed up to vote at the nomination meeting. But our dirty little secret was that, if the central party favoured one candidate over another, it could fix things to give that candidate the advantage. The old system was subject to real abuse. I wanted to end that. The best nomination processes needed active, open, and honest engagement from the riding associations and the central party. I was determined to make that happen. After months of consultation led by party stalwarts Tricia Waldron and Gord Phaneuf, the party adopted a wholesale revision of the rules. The new system required that a riding association submit a nomination plan with full details of who the candidates would be, the cut-off date for memberships, and where and when the nomination meeting would take place. Then the riding president, the party's regional vice-president, and the "nominations commissioner" (an appointee of the leader) would have to approve the plan.

We also needed to recognize that the central campaign had an abiding interest in the overall makeup of the team. So the new rules gave the leader the right to appoint candidates in up to five ridings. That meant those candidates wouldn't have to contest their nominations. The appointment power would give the party the ability to strengthen the overall mix of candidates with the assurance that the appointee would be on the ballot.

Madeleine Meilleur was at the top of that list. She was a francophone woman, a lawyer, a nurse, a municipal politician — an ideal candidate. On our advice, Dalton appointed her as the candidate for Ottawa-Vanier. It wasn't that Madeleine wasn't prepared to fight for a nomination. She was. But we weren't prepared to take a chance on losing her. We did the same for Linda Jeffrey in Brampton Centre, Brad Duguid in Scarborough Centre, Tony Wong in Markham, and Shafiq Qaadri in Etobicoke North.

Some fifteen months into my tenure as party president a tragic event took place that changed my life dramatically. On March 24, 2001, Al Palladini, my successor in the riding I had represented for ten years, died of a sudden heart attack on a golf course while vacationing in Mexico.

Al and I had been friends. We were baseball teammates in 1993 at the Toronto Blue Jays Fantasy Camp in Dunedin, Florida. When Mike Harris approached him about being the Progressive Conservative candidate in my old riding, he sought my advice.

He wanted to be quite sure I wasn't going to run before he threw his hat in the ring. Al had the status of an icon throughout Woodbridge and beyond. He was the ideal candidate for Harris in York Centre. When we met, I reassured him that I would not be a candidate and left him with these observations to consider: First, I told him he would win. I felt that Ontario was in the process of making a sharp turn to the right and would ultimately embrace Harris's message of lower taxes and smaller government, and that the Tories would win a majority. Second, he needed to be assured of a Cabinet job. Life as a government backbencher should not be his goal. And third, I warned that if he did become a minister, he could not even set foot in his car dealership again so long as he was in Cabinet.

As it turned out, Al Palladini paid a heavy price for entering public life. He did win York Centre by almost nine thousand votes and, coincidentally (no doubt!), he became Harris's minister of transportation. But the car dealership never survived his political career. Its success was rooted in Al Palladini's effervescent personality. Without him it began to fail. I'm convinced his early death at age fifty-seven came from a combination of the pressures of government, a very stressful divorce, and the loss of so much of the value he'd created in his car dealership.

I was in Dunedin, Florida, enjoying the Blue Jays' spring training camp, when I heard about what had happened to Al. I was well into my second year as party president and soon to become chair of the election campaign. The day after Al's death, Ian Urquhart, the Queen's Park columnist for the *Toronto Star,* tracked me down and asked whether I was interested in reclaiming my old seat. I told him I actually thought it was inconsistent with my job as party president to be an MPP as well. Later that month the party held an "ideas conference" in Niagara-on-the-Lake. I spent most of my time at that conference sequestered in my hotel room, trying to avoid those who would be urging me to run. Then the phone rang.

"Dalton wants to talk to you," said the voice at the other end. We met for about thirty minutes.

His message was clear.

"Greg, you have to run," the leader said. "We have to have that seat back."

I didn't have a worthy rebuttal. We did have to have that seat back, and I was almost certainly the person most likely to win it back for our side. As party president, I had been urging people to do whatever it would take to prepare us for the next election. I realized that the same rule would have to apply to me.

I also saw a broader storyline. Less than a year earlier there had been another by-election in Ancaster-Dundas-Flamborough-Aldershot, a suburban Hamilton riding. The Liberals' Ted McMeekin won it. I figured, if I can take back my old riding (now called Vaughan-King-Aurora), the Liberals' momentum would be very significant.

So I was back in, and with a vengeance. It was in equal measure exhilarating and terrifying. From the moment the by-election was called I remembered how much I relished the challenges of campaigning and winning. I had left the riding six years earlier on very good terms with my constituency. It almost felt as if an older political warrior was being given a warm welcome back to the battlefield. Volunteers came from ridings across the province to ensure that every door was visited and every voter canvassed.

Certainly there were risks that made me fret. I was now a rather high-profile party president and the recently announced chair of the next general election campaign, whenever it might be called. Were I to lose the by-election it would be a brutal blow to our party's future electability. We simply had to win.

More frightful still was the sharp turn in my life that returning to Queen's Park would cause. Before Al's death, the plan had been to work like crazy to win the election for Dalton — I was anticipating a general election sometime in 2002 — and then return to the luxury of private life. Now I realized in all likelihood I would win the by-election and thereafter be a significant player in Dalton McGuinty's first Cabinet. It was a shock to the system indeed.

Just after I announced my candidacy, the Mike Harris government did something that seemed ideologically inconsistent with everything they'd done in the past. They introduced a bill to protect the Oak Ridges Moraine, an ecologically significant area of almost two thousand square kilometres that went right through my riding. Years before, a group of lively environmentalists had come together to establish the STORM (Save the Oak Ridges Moraine) coalition, headed by Debbe Crandall. STORM had been working for years to secure legislative protection for the moraine. But the Tories had done nothing to encourage the movement.

Suddenly, confronted by a tough by-election, the Tories found religion in the form of the Oak Ridges Moraine Act. Then, Liberal MPP Mike Colle, who had worked for years with STORM, did something quite unusual. On the day that the bill was introduced he rose in the chamber and asked for unanimous consent for the bill to be given first, second, and third reading that very day. Not surprisingly, given that the by-election hung in the balance, the government agreed. It was a glorious and instant victory for the advocates of moraine preservation, but politically it did not lift the Tories' fortunes in York Region one iota. Indeed, Mike Colle and the Ontario Liberals were given the lion's share of the political credit for the moraine victory.

The Vaughan-King-Aurora by-election took place on June 28, 2001, almost sixteen years to the day after the Peterson government (including a youngish minister of colleges and universities) was sworn in — the first Liberal government in forty-two years. And it would prove to be twice lucky for me. I defeated my PC opponent, Joyce Frustaglio, with 61 percent of the votes cast, an overwhelming mandate.

Things began to move very quickly after the by-election. First on the agenda was to establish a constituency office that could handle the lion's share of local issues, given that much of my time would be taken up with the coming general election. Next was moving out of The Sorbara Group and into an office on the main floor of the legislative assembly building, and finally getting back to preparing the party to win the remaining 102 ridings in the province. On top of that list was continuing with the search for candidates.

Looking for candidates is a bit like scouting for a 103-member baseball team. You look for talent. Then you evaluate it. Then you test it. You develop a sixth sense when you meet prospective candidates. Can they do the job? Can they win? Are they personable? And are they overly ambitious?

As the lead-up to the 2003 general election continued, we found our new nomination process was working well. We did run into a bit of a crisis in the riding of Bramalea-Gore-Malton. Shortly before the nominating meeting, we learned that one candidate, Dr. Kuldip Kular, had been disciplined by the College of Physicians and Surgeons of Ontario for inappropriately prescribing drugs to a patient ten years earlier. The CPSO had launched an inquiry into the matter and Kular had been disciplined. I invited Kular to Queen's Park for a chat.

"Kuldip, you're a great guy, but you can't run for a Liberal nomination," I told him.

He didn't take it well. In fact, he said he'd fight my ruling, and he did. He went out, signed up a ton of members, and proceeded to contest the nomination as if our meeting had never taken place. So our party's "nominations working group" did some more digging. We talked to our contacts in the Sikh community and the local riding association who assured us, "If Kuldip wins the nomination, he'll win the general election." So we backed off. Kular did win the nomination, and on election night he carried the seat by almost four thousand votes.

As part of the overall candidate search, two other cases warrant mention. In 1999, Harinder Takhar tried to win a Liberal nomination in one of the Mississauga ridings. He believed the party manipulated the process to deny him a possible victory. So in 2003 he came to me to complain. "Harinder," I told him, "I'll make one promise to you this time. You'll get a fair shot. There will be no manipulation." Takhar took my word for it, won the nomination, and then carried the election by almost three thousand votes. Mario Racco had the same complaint in Thornhill. He felt he had been abused by the Liberal Party brass in 1999. I took him out to lunch and assured him things were different. "I guarantee you a fair chance to get nominated this time," I told him. He didn't believe me. I persisted. "Give it a try. You'll see."

Mario won his nomination and eked out a victory on election night by eight hundred votes.

All of our campaign preparations were at full throttle when, just before Thanksgiving in the fall of 2001, another bombshell dropped. To everyone's surprise, Premier Mike Harris announced that he would be stepping down as premier as soon as his party could choose a successor. Suddenly there was a whole new dynamic at play.

As the PC candidates for the leadership came forward, I thought Ernie Eves, who'd retired from politics, would be the hardest contender to defeat. He was a Conservative but was seen as a Red Tory, without Harris's harsh edges. He had a commendable record as finance minister and was well respected. Sure enough, Eves won his party's leadership in March 2002, and relatively easily, on the second ballot.

Eves was popular when he took over. So we needed to tie him to the previous unpopularity of Mike Harris. Our plan was simple: we would constantly refer to the Tories as the "Harris-Eves Government." Mercifully, it stuck.

There's no hard and fast rule about political transitions. The question of when to go to the polls is one of the hardest any new first minister has to deal with. John Turner called an election just ten days after winning the prime ministership in 1984. He believed the bump he got in the polls was real. It wasn't. He found himself on the losing end of the biggest majority government in Canadian history. Similarly, Frank Miller called an election three months after becoming premier in 1985 and found himself on the opposition benches shortly thereafter. However, William Davis won the PC leadership in February 1971 and then increased the size of the Tories' majority in October.

The truth was that after Harris left I was nervous. We weren't ready to contest an election. There was a lot of money still to be raised. Our policy platform wasn't nearly ready to go. My suspicion to this day is that, had Ernie Eves called a snap election for the spring of 2002, capitalizing on his convention popularity and the strong core of PC support, we again would have been on the losing end of a general election; we never would have heard of Premier Dalton McGuinty. But Eves took a pass on a snap post-convention election and we were especially grateful.

With the nomination process much improved, the next big fix was fund-raising. This had never been our strong suit. We tended to do the same things every year: we held the Heritage Dinner, followed by letters and phone calls around election time. Then a saviour arrived, sent by what could only have been divine intervention. Greg Wong had good Liberal roots and was busily raising money for CAMH — the Centre for Addiction and Mental Health in Toronto. I wanted him raising money for *us*. Greg agreed, provided he could have complete control of the operation. "No problem," I told him. "Go for it."

Greg created the Ontario Liberal Fund, with separate offices away from party's head office at 10 St. Mary Street in downtown Toronto. He wanted to have an independent mission, right down to hiring his own people, and developing a visible Ontario Liberal Fund brand. Organizationally, this turned out to be a home run.

Political fundraising invariably gives rise to controversy. Each jurisdiction in Canada has its own rules, and each party can shape its fundraising within those rules. Ontario's law sets out very strict limits on donations and requires full disclosure of donors' names. Historically, it has permitted donations from Ontario residents and from corporations and trade unions with an Ontario presence.

Early in 2002 the federal Liberals pursued a different course. Prime Minister Jean Chrétien wanted to clean up the rules around fundraising. His Liberal majority government passed a new law forbidding corporations and unions from donating to political parties. Only individuals henceforth could donate. Stephen LeDrew, the federal party president at the time, called the change "dumb as a sack of hammers." No political reward ever came from that change. Well before that, some Ontario Liberals were urging that we voluntarily eliminate donations from corporations. Indeed, caucus was on the verge of passing just such a resolution when I heard about the move. I asked to speak to caucus in my capacity as party president and campaign chair. "I have just completed our presentation to the bankers to secure a loan for the next election," I told them. "If you do this, our loan application will be rejected and there will be no money for the next campaign. No bank will lend us money if we tell them we plan to cut off our primary source of funds. I cannot let this happen on my watch."

I certainly was not threatening to resign. But I needed to make the point in no uncertain terms that voluntarily forgoing our major source of revenue might have some appeal to a small segment of the electorate and media, but most voters would care little, and we certainly would not be able to fund the coming election in any reasonable way. We were still $5 million in debt from the 1999 election and needed to demonstrate to our bankers not only that we could pay it back, but also that we were a good risk for the 2003 campaign. I left the caucus room after my presentation and was advised within a short time that the proposal was no longer on the table.

Most important, from a campaign point of view, a strong group of advisers was working tirelessly on a comprehensive platform that would touch virtually all important policy areas within provincial jurisdiction: health care, social services, justice policy, environmental proposals, fiscal management, taxation, transit, urban finance, northern development, support for cultural industries, government transparency, and government advertising. The list went on. We developed a plan to publish our proposals one after another as the finishing touches were put on each. I was very proud of the work this team did, even if I was somewhat concerned about our eventual ability to deliver on all of the plans.

Most difficult of all was the fact that we were up against a clock we did not control — the timing of the next election. Ontario at this point still had no fixed election date law. The dissolution of Parliament and calling an election were still the divine right of the premier to decide. It was entirely in the hands of Ernie Eves. So we crossed our fingers and toes and hoped the fates would buy us the time we desperately needed to get our act together.

Strangely enough, they did just that.

5

Choosing Change: The 2003 Election

Was Ernie Eves unbeatable in the spring of 2002? I was deeply concerned that he was. But things started to happen that gave me some comfort. After Eves was sworn in as Ontario's twenty-third premier in April, he immediately became a candidate in a by-election so he could lead his PC government from the legislature. Eves had left politics in early 2001 and, with his victory at the Progressive Conservative leadership convention, was the first Ontarian in almost a century to become premier *without* a seat in the legislature.

As a rule, when a party leader who doesn't have a seat tries to get one, he finds the safest seat he can, and it's normally a slam-dunk victory. The previous occupant of the seat Eves would run in — Dufferin-Peel-Wellington-Grey — was David Tilson, and he won it in 1999 with 65 percent of the vote. So it certainly looked as if Eves would glide to victory there.

What could we possibly do to make that ride a little rougher? My fellow MPP and friend Mike Colle and my protégé Steven Del Duca had an idea. They knew a bright, passionate, young environmentalist from Toronto named Josh Matlow. "We should get Josh to run there," they suggested.

I loved the idea. My assistant Nicole Miller tracked down Josh in France, where he was vacationing with his mother. We had a very short phone conversation.

"Josh, how'd you like to be our candidate in the upcoming by-election against Ernie Eves?" I asked.

"I'd love to," was his immediate reply.

"How soon can you be back?" I then asked.

"Gimme twenty-four hours," said Josh. We had a candidate.

Josh ran a fabulous campaign, filled with the passion for which he was so well known. He had no real roots in the riding but he fell in love with it — all the while blasting Eves for his proposal to sell off Hydro One, the province's newly created electricity transmission company. Everywhere he went, people told Josh, "We don't know you that well but we don't like this Hydro One business, so you have our votes."

On by-election night, early returns actually had Matlow in the lead for a while. By the end of the night, Eves won the seat, but only by 3,500 votes. Almost 20 percent of Tilson's previous vote had evaporated. We had dramatically cut into the Tories' support in perhaps the safest Conservative seat in the province. A good omen.

And there was more good news. On the same night, there was another by-election in Mike Harris's former riding of Nipissing. Although the Tories held that seat, too, they saw Harris's margin of victory from 1999 — nearly three thousand votes — almost completely disappear. The PCs' by-election candidate, Al McDonald, won by just *nineteen votes*. With our two previous by-election wins (Ted McMeekin's in 2000 and mine in 2001), and these two close calls in 2002, I was becoming more confident about the possibilities of a Dalton McGuinty victory down the road.

As these by-election campaigns progressed, the political professionals in our party warned me that I was spending too much time on the Matlow race and not enough in Nipissing, where they felt we actually had a chance to win. I had become enamoured of the idea of knocking off the new premier and did spend a disproportionate amount of time there. Had I listened to our people, been more realistic about our prospects, and spent more time in Nipissing, I'm convinced we'd have won that seat. I'm still ticked at myself about this one. In fact, one day I was on my way to North Bay to lend a hand to the campaign, but by the time I got to Orillia a huge thunderstorm began to brew. So I turned the car around, and never made it. If only …

In politics, if you lose by five thousand votes, well, it really isn't your fault. There wasn't much you could have done. But if you lose by fifty votes, well then, it *is* your fault. A little more effort would have meant a win rather than a loss. Our nineteen-vote loss in Nipissing felt like my fault, and the wizards on our central campaign team did nothing to disabuse me of that notion.

Ernie Eves was now back in the legislature, and our task on the opposition side of the House was to be ready whenever the next election call came. My concern about a snap call would prove unnecessary; as 2002 turned into 2003 and still no election call, we got the time we needed to prepare. But then a mixture of the fates and some extremely poor judgment began to doom the Tories' prospects for re-election. In February 2003 something most of us had never heard of descended on Ontario: severe acute respiratory syndrome, known as SARS. More than eight hundred people worldwide, and forty-four in Ontario, would succumb to this dreaded condition. Our health-care system was unprepared to deal with it.

Then, a month later, a self-inflicted wound harmed Tory fortunes further. For some reason, the Eves government decided to present its first budget *not* in the Ontario legislature, but rather at a Magna automotive training facility in York Region. It was an inexplicable decision and went over like a lead balloon. The Tories took a daily hammering in the media, and if there were plans to go to the people after that budget, those plans were now off. At this point, it didn't matter anymore. We felt that the momentum was with us. Then one more disaster befell the Tories: the lights went out. Literally. In mid-August 2003, all over the northeast of North America, ten million Ontarians and forty-five million Americans suffered through the second-most widespread power failure in history. Some Progressive Conservatives thought this was great political news, that it would give Eves an opportunity to show off his leadership abilities. Maybe so. But it also gave us the chance to hammer away at how the PCs had let our energy infrastructure degrade over the past decade.

When Ernie Eves finally called the election on September 2 for a vote a month later on October 2, 2003, we looked and felt like a party ready to take over — if we could avoid any major mistakes. Everything was different than it had been in 1999. Dalton was a much more effective leader; our coffers were flush, and we had a definitive body of proposals in our platform.

Over the previous year we had worked feverishly for this moment.

Our campaign committee, made up of some sixty party stalwarts, had met monthly for over a year in a downtown law office.

A smaller group of advisers known as "the Leader's Circle" — so called because the leader both attended and chaired the meetings — had also met monthly for over a year. This group, which included Don Guy, Phil Dewan, Gordon Ashworth, Greg Wong, Helen Burstyn, Gerald Butts, Bob Lopinski, Matt Maychak, Dave Gene, Dave Pryce, Sharon Laredo, Peter Wilkinson, David McNaughton, Ross McGregor, and myself, oversaw all aspects of the campaign.

The party staff had built strong election organizations in most of the province's ridings. Over the previous year it had held campaign colleges and regional training sessions for all those who would be responsible for preparing and managing local campaigns. Campaign managers and individual riding campaigns developed their strategic plans to take into account the specific issues in each community around the province. Almost every first-time candidate had received a thorough media training course that emphasized what not to say as well as what to say and how to say it.

On the central front, we completed preparations for the war room — the daily issues response team. It was up and running within hours of the election call. Those responsible for the Leader's Tour had a full agenda and a message track for each day of the campaign, with enough flexibility to shift gears if the situation warranted. The party platform had been fully publicized and decisions made as to where to shine the brightest spotlight on our proposals. Campaign calling cards, brochures, buttons, and posters were ready and shipped out when the call came.

We had arranged for full funding of the campaign and secured a team of volunteers to work the fundraising phones every day of the campaign. The media buy had also been completed, with additional resources in our coffers should they be needed in the campaign's last days. We had built an advertising campaign around the slogan "Choose Change": we made it part of every communication initiative.

It brought joy to my heart, as campaign chair and party president, to see how efficiently the talent of hundreds and hundreds of campaign workers had been organized into a powerful piece of political machinery. Through all this shone the handiwork of the campaign director, Don Guy, and the campaign manager, Dave Gene, both of whom had a profound commitment to Dalton.

Our determination to win had permeated every dimension of the campaign and every campaign worker.

For all our preparations, we were also the beneficiaries of some lucky breaks. One such break occurred in the riding of Stoney Creek. We had nominated a candidate named Tony Magnini. But he became embroiled in fraud allegations after the election had been called. This was a disaster in the making. Our opponent was the Progressive Conservatives' Brad Clark, who was a cabinet minister. We told Magnini he had to stand down, that he could no longer be our candidate. So there we were, the election called, with no candidate in the riding of Stoney Creek. Our campaign there seemed dead in the water.

And then Dave Gene, the party's campaign manager, suggested Jennifer Mossop, the well-known and, more importantly, well-liked television news anchor from Hamilton. When I went to meet Jennifer she admitted interest in running, but she said there was one big problem: she had a three-month-old baby and couldn't see how she could both run for office and take care of her infant at the same time.

"Indira Gandhi had a baby while she was prime minister of India," I told her. "You can do this." Sure enough, Jennifer got in and figured it out. She had a minibus to which she would retreat while on the hustings, to take the time to nurse her baby and then get right back out there. It seemed as if every door she knocked on, people met her and said, "Hey, it's Jennifer. We've always wanted to meet you." Early on we had written off Stoney Creek. Instead, Jennifer Mossop would go on to knock off a sitting cabinet minister.

One of the biggest changes between 1999 and 2003 was in the area of advertising. We all remembered well the Tory ads from '99, which claimed that Dalton "wasn't up to the job." For some reason, despite ample evidence to the contrary, the PCs went with the same advertising theme in 2003, claiming Dalton "*still* wasn't up to the job." Big mistake. People were no longer buying it.

Dalton's campaign abilities had improved dramatically — almost to the point of rock star status. He was comfortable, at ease, and engaging wherever he went. And his wife Terri, who was with him almost every day, was seen as a beautiful, charming, and thoughtful candidate for the spouse of an Ontario premier.

Peter Byrne was the creative mind responsible for our ad campaign. He was terrific. The geeky, awkward Opposition leader of 1999 had been transformed into a confident, sincere premier-in-waiting, and it showed. One ad featured footage of McGuinty on the stump, speaking inspirationally, appealing to the better angels in us all, and ending with our campaign slogan: "Choose Change." That phrase said it all.

As September began, we actually entered the campaign with a lead, but by the end of the first week our polling showed it had disappeared.

And then we caught another break.

At the end of the second week of the campaign, the Tories issued a press release no doubt intended to be funny. But few people interpreted it that way. The release referred to McGuinty as an "evil reptilian kitten-eater from another planet." We were overjoyed and pounced on this significant mistake, which seemed to remind everyone how mean-spirited and negative the Tories were. We even had fun with it. Don Guy and Dave Gene got T-shirts made up saying, "Call me an evil reptilian kitten eater, I want smaller class sizes." Or "Call me an evil reptilian kitten eater, I want better health care." It was the turning point of the campaign. Across the province we now felt an enormous sense of momentum.

The next major milestone was the leader's debate. The general consensus was that Dalton had been hammered badly in Debate 1999. We were determined to have him much better prepared for Debate 2003, and he was. This time around he exuded a confidence that was noted by all the pundits, including those who were not anxious to see him win. Both Ernie Eves and Howard Hampton tried separately to "mark him up," but it was to no avail.

It was also to our advantage that Ernie Eves ran on a much harder right-wing platform than his personal politics seemed to indicate. It was mostly Mike Harris's team that ran the Eves' campaign, except that Mike Harris wasn't the leader. Too much of what came out of Eves' mouth seemed inauthentic. It was as if he were running for a third Harris term.

As for Howard Hampton, it was clear from the get-go that this was to be a Liberal/Conservative battle. While Hampton campaigned diligently, there seemed to be no joy or sense of mission in what the NDP was proposing.

As election night approached we knew that we would win a majority. The only question was how large the margin would be. In the end it was not close. Liberals won seventy-two seats — a strong majority — and almost twice the number we had at dissolution. The Tories held on to twenty-four seats to become the Official Opposition, and the NDP went from nine seats to seven to remain the third party but lost their official party status under the rules of the legislature.

My first stop after the polls closed was the Masonic Temple in midtown Toronto to celebrate with the central campaign team. It was bedlam. The joy in that room was something I've rarely experienced. Then I headed to my riding to celebrate our local victory. I didn't speak to or see the premier-elect that night, since he was in Ottawa celebrating there.

A memorable moment in the victory's aftermath happened the next day on the front lawn of Queen's Park. I saw Matt Maychak, the former journalist, who'd become our communications guru because he so deeply believed in and frankly loved Dalton McGuinty. Matt is normally a pretty straight-ahead, unemotional guy with a wicked sense of humour. But that day he just grabbed me, hugged me, and started to cry.

"I just wanted to thank you," he said. "We could never have done this without you."

"It was about the team, Matt," I countered. "We had a great team."

It wasn't until the following day that I got a phone call from the man who would become Ontario's twenty-fourth premier. It was a brief but important call for both of us. I told him that he had done a super job carrying the campaign to every corner of the province, with style and grace and energy. We agreed that the real work was about to begin. Then with warmness that I had rarely felt from him, he thanked me for my role in the campaign and said we would compare notes soon.

And we did. After all, there was a swearing-in ceremony to prepare for, a Cabinet to appoint, and a mission to complete.

When my first tour of Cabinet duty came to an end in 1990, I was hardly what you'd call a heavy hitter. I started out in 1985 with an interesting, middle-of-the-pack job in Cabinet —minister of colleges and universities, and minister of skills development. I got promoted to a tougher job, but one that I found challenging and invigorating, not to mention one of government's mainline ministries — Labour. Then I got "reassigned" to consumer and commercial relations. By the time we Liberals were out of office, I was really quite an insignificant player and suspected that my time in an Ontario Cabinet had come to an end.

And yet, politics is a business that consistently provides unanticipated surprises. Thirteen years after that 1990 election debacle, I found myself in a completely different position. I was now one of a small group of advisers whose mission it was to help the premier-designate craft his first Cabinet. We began our work within two weeks of the election.

Before the meetings began, I had a very personal chat with Dalton.

"I don't need to be in this new Cabinet. My job was to help you get elected premier," I said to him. "But if you want me in it will have to be the finance ministry. I am simply not interested in anything else."

That may have sounded a tad arrogant, but the premier understood the point I was making. I had come back into politics in 1999 to get Dalton McGuinty elected. That mission was fulfilled. I had done what I set out to do. So I just told Dalton I would not be offended if he, too, decided that I had completed my mission and found someone else for finance.

His reply was classic McGuinty: "I hear ya." He kept his options open as a good leader would. After all, Scarborough MPP Gerry Phillips, who was first elected in 1987, had been an excellent finance critic during our time in opposition. And I also knew MPP Dwight Duncan from Windsor was interested in the job. I didn't want my personal ambition to tie McGuinty's hands. By saying what I'd said, I recognized it was possible I'd be out of Cabinet altogether, because I really wasn't interested in doing any other job.

And so the meetings began. Hour after hour, we gathered to discuss who would form the new Cabinet. It was remarkably collegial. I don't recall a single raised voice or harsh disagreement. There was an immediate consensus that I would be the finance minister. I breathed no sigh of relief when that happened, but I do remember thinking that I was taking on a role I could not have imagined in 1999 when I signed on as a volunteer party president.

One of Ontario's great premiers, William Davis, once said that Cabinet-making was the hardest thing he ever did in public life. He found it extremely difficult to tell friends who'd been with him through thick and thin, "No, I'm sorry, you didn't make it into Cabinet." Or to tell them, "I have to drop you from Cabinet." Now I was engaged in the same process, although it would be left to the new premier and his chief of staff to deliver the good and bad news. No one played personal favourites. No one went to bat for someone who was clearly unqualified to be in. Our recommendations were based on who could do the job well.

Getting this right was especially important, since McGuinty had been hammered in the past for making some questionable appointments. After becoming leader in 1996 his first hire was his brother Brendan, who was eminently qualified to be the leader's chief of staff. But Dalton faced a barrage of criticism from those who thought his first act ought not to be offering patronage to a family member. Brendan was let go almost as quickly as he was hired. Then there was Joe Cordiano. McGuinty made Joe deputy leader, since he was the kingmaker at 4:30 in the morning on December 1, 1996, bringing 85 percent of his delegates to McGuinty. This move allowed him to win the leadership convention on the fifth ballot. But somewhere along the way, McGuinty and Cordiano got off the rails. Dalton fired him as deputy leader and earned more bad publicity. It was all the more important to get this first Cabinet just right.

We understood, then, that Cabinet-making is one of the really great and delicate arts in politics. Essentially, you start with a list of all the names of the MPPs who are slam-dunks to be ministers. Then you make a list of all the people who under no circumstances should go into Cabinet. Then you've got a final list of those MPPs who are "on the bubble." They have some things going for them, but perhaps not enough to get a place at the Cabinet table.

The leader made one thing clear at the outset. "Everyone who ran against me for the party leadership is going to be in Cabinet," he said. Of course, he didn't mean absolutely everyone; not Greg Kells, who came last on the first ballot with just twenty-four votes and disappeared from politics after that. And he certainly didn't mean Anna-Marie Castrilli, who was a one-term Liberal MPP from 1995 to 1999, and then ran for the Progressive Conservatives in the 1999 election. No, what he meant was that Gerard Kennedy, Joe Cordiano, Dwight Duncan, and John Gerretsen would all have to be in, and no heed was paid to who supported whom at that extraordinary leadership convention.

Again, there was a quick consensus on some assignments. Kennedy was an easy fit for education. Cordiano had shown some real strengths, but his relationship with McGuinty concerned some. Joe had been an MPP since 1985, but he never made it into Cabinet under David Peterson. This time he would make it. McGuinty made him minister for economic development and trade — a solid, senior portfolio. Gerretsen, as a former mayor of Kingston, was a natural for municipal affairs. Duncan, an energetic guy and a proven performer in the House, went to energy.

McGuinty added another proviso: there would be no extra consideration given to the small number of MPPs that supported him at the 1996 convention. Merit was the prime consideration.

"We have a higher mission here," was how the leader put it. He wanted a small, representative, effective team. That was bad news for Tony Ruprecht, a veteran downtown Toronto MPP who was in Peterson's Cabinet back in the 1980s and one of the early supporters of Dalton's leadership bid. He didn't make the cut this time.

Of course, the first list is easy to make, and it was abundantly clear amongst our group whom we *had to have* in Cabinet. For example, Michael Bryant was an easy choice for attorney general. He was a lawyer who had clerked at the Supreme Court of Canada. (We didn't know at the time that Michael was battling the demons of alcoholism. Had we known, I suspect that would have been enough to render him unsuitable.) Sudbury's Rick Bartolucci had been a champion of Ontario's north since his first election in 1995. He was a perfect fit for northern development and mines.

Monte Kwinter, now the oldest MPP ever and a legend even a decade ago, took community safety and correctional services. David Caplan was a second-generation politician, his mother Elinor having been both a David Peterson and Jean Chrétien cabinet minister. David had great political skills, so he was put into the important new portfolio of public infrastructure renewal. We also knew that we were going to damage our relations with the Jewish community when we would retroactively take back the private school tax credit the Tories had offered; having him as another member of that community in Cabinet, we thought, might help.

Steve Peters wasn't a farmer but he was from St. Thomas, the heart of agriculture country, and he knew the agriculture file well — so he was a great fit for agriculture and food. Jim Bradley was the dean of the caucus, having been elected in 1977. He was another ex-minister from the Peterson days. We knew Jim needed to be in Cabinet, but the premier wanted him in a somewhat lower-profile portfolio, thus tourism and recreation. The class act and team player that he is, Jim never complained that he wasn't given his beloved ministry of the environment; it was eventually a position he returned to following the 2011 election campaign.

Gerry Phillips wouldn't get finance despite having been a great critic. But his knowledge of the state of the province's books would be invaluable as chair of the management board of Cabinet, which scrutinizes every government expenditure. We knew Sandra Pupatello had to be in Cabinet. She was a dynamic woman and a great performer. We also knew she wouldn't be thrilled with community and social services. She wasn't, and she let us know it. David Ramsay was another MPP who went back to the Peterson days. As a northern member, he was a good fit for natural resources. Madeleine Meilleur was a sure bet to get in. She had municipal political experience, she was a francophone and a woman, and she represented eastern Ontario. One of the most elegant MPPs I've ever served with, Madeleine was a great fit in the culture portfolio; she was also made minister for francophone affairs. These were the easy choices.

I'd always considered Mike Colle, the midtown Toronto MPP, a great friend and ally. I thought his work preserving the Oak Ridges Moraine was terrific. He had been chairman of the Toronto Transit Commission. But I couldn't get him into Cabinet. When I pitched his name there was just no pickup around the table. Others said we already had enough Toronto and "Italian" representation. But I was happy when my suggestion that he become my parliamentary assistant at finance was accepted by the group. We subsequently learned to work well together.

The executive council also has to *look like* Ontario. So we had some hard decisions to make concerning MPPs from distinctive cultural communities, even if they were new members without a lot of political or parliamentary experience. The Sikh community, for example, had become a crucial base of support for Ontario Liberals, so rookie MPP Harinder

Takhar was a logical choice as transportation minister over other MPPs who had already served a term or two in parliament. We had one black member of caucus, the Jamaican-born rookie Mary Anne Chambers. She was a superstar, and I was thrilled that she was assigned to my old port-folios, now called training, colleges, and universities. She could have suc-ceeded in any number of portfolios, having been a senior vice-president at Scotiabank, a member of the governing council at the University of Toronto, and a board member of the United Way of Greater Toronto. But the new premier wasn't prepared to be a slave to ethnicity. For example, Peter Fonseca could have become the first ever Liberal cabinet minister from the Portuguese community. But not yet. Tony Wong was the only MPP in our caucus from the Chinese-Canadian community. But he wasn't selected, either.

Geography is important for every "Cabinet-maker," and one of our hardest decisions focused on who would represent southwestern Ontario. We had John Milloy from Kitchener, and Deb Matthews, Chris Bentley, and Khalil Ramal from London. I was particularly attracted to the idea of getting Deb Matthews into Cabinet. I'd encouraged her to run and knew she'd be good. Ultimately, it came down to Matthews vs. Bentley, and there was simply more support in the room for Chris. He became labour minister. Deb eventually replaced me as party president, despite the advice of her brother-in-law, former premier David Peterson, who urged her not to do it! He was worried that being both an MPP and the party president would be too demanding. I told her otherwise: "Deb, this will be a stepping stone into Cabinet for you. You'll be able to develop a province-wide profile. You'll visit every corner of Ontario. And it'll give you a political reach beyond the barbecue circuit in London. Besides, you'll love it." Sure enough, Deb served the party very well as my successor and after the 2007 election was sworn in as minister for children and youth services, and minister of women's issues. Two years after that she earned a huge promotion, an appointment to health and long-term care. And after Kathleen Wynne became premier in 2013, Deb added deputy premier to her list of assignments. It all worked out pretty well.

Speaking of Kathleen Wynne, I went to that first meeting with her on my list as community and social services minister. She was a first-time MPP, and I really liked her. But it quickly became apparent there was just not enough support for her elsewhere in the room. Besides, we already had plenty of Toronto representation. So Wynne would have to wait. Three years later, she had obviously impressed enough people that she went straight into the education portfolio to succeed Gerard Kennedy and to become one of the best we ever had.

Interestingly, my first significant disagreement with the premier-designate centred on who should be health minister. McGuinty had Leona Dombrowsky, the one-term MPP from Hastings-Frontenac-Lennox and Addington, on his list. As much as I liked Leona personally, I thought this impossibly hard job needed to go to someone with more political chops.

"I think it should be George Smitherman," I said to the gathering. "He's clearly established his political skills and his skills in the House. He helped establish the commitment to reduce auto insurance premiums. He's one of the strongest members of our caucus." I started seeing heads nod; without a great deal more discussion it was agreed that George would be our first minister of health and long-term care. It was arguably the most important — and controversial — decision we would make. In opposition, George had been an attack dog with a keen political sense. The question was whether he could translate those skills into effective oversight of the largest and most important ministry in government.

Our objectives in health for that first term — and the mandate we were about to hand to George — were daunting. We began by investing significant new resources for hip and knee replacements and for cataract surgery. We launched a program to reduce wait times, and eventually designed and implemented a wait-times strategy that allowed patients to track the wait times at facilities across the province. We developed a long overdue regional system for health-care planning with fourteen new Local Health Integration Networks. We designed and funded new Family Health Teams to increase access to family doctors. We added desperately needed resources to home care. A series of new community health centres were approved and funded. Thousands of nurses were added to the system, and work began on the recognition of a new category of nurse — the nurse practitioner, who would take on responsibilities previously restricted to doctors. Midwifery became a fully funded part of birthing across the province. Funds were directed to hospital emergency rooms to reduce chronically long waits. And billions of dollars were authorized to support the most aggressive era of hospital construction and reconstruction in the history of the province.

George took up the mandate with passion and dispatch. He showed remarkable leadership arguing repeatedly at the Cabinet table and around the province that more effective and more cost efficient health care must be the government's number one priority. But his tenure was not without controversy. He tolerated no challenge to his mission and the style with which he approached it. And during his time in health, two issues arose — overspending and expense abuse in the eHealth Ontario initiative and a shocking abuse of authority at the senior levels of Ornge, Ontario's air ambulance service program — both of which caused endless headaches for his successors in the health ministry and the government in general.

Believe it or not, one new member of the caucus actually lobbied me *not* to be in Cabinet. Linda Jeffrey was someone I courted mercilessly to run for us. I made several trips to Brampton, where she was the municipal budget chief on Brampton city council, to convince her to run. But she was very reluctant. Eventually I prevailed, and thankfully she won, but only by a thousand votes. After the election, Linda told me: "I don't want to be in Cabinet. I need to learn how this place works. I hope one day to be good enough and I hope you'll keep tutoring me in the meantime." It took more than six years, but eventually, Linda Jeffrey was sworn in as minister of natural resources in January 2010. I was somewhat saddened for the Liberals under Premier Wynne when Linda left Queen's Park to contest the mayor's job in her home community of Brampton.

Cabinet-making is hard. For every person you appoint, you break the hearts of many others. But it was done. And the new McGuinty ministry was sworn in on October 23, 2003. It was among the best that ever served Ontario.

On November 20 the new administration opened the thirty-eighth parliament with a Speech from the Throne that set out our priorities for the first session. After that day of pageantry it was down to work. My assignment was to find a solution to the fiscal mess we had inherited from our predecessors.

6

A Finance Minister's Treasury

With the Throne Speech out of the way, the entire Liberal caucus got down to the real work of government. Our mission was straightforward: to be hard-working public servants dedicated to improving the public services for thirteen million Ontarians.

My first assignment was to present *Ontario's Economic Outlook and Fiscal Review*, also known as the Fall Economic Statement. It included a corporate tax increase and the cancellation of the private school tax credit, which the Tories had implemented and we had campaigned against.

But the life of a finance minister means being involved in virtually everything a government does, and each year to present a budget that sets out in clear detail the government's full agenda for that year and beyond.

I do not propose here to review in detail all the trials and tribulations of a finance minister, but rather to look at three initiatives that defined my time in the treasury.

The first, the Ontario Health Premium, was surely the most painful. The other two, the York subway extension and the Ontario Child Benefit, will have a lasting effect on the lives of Ontarians for years to come.

The Ontario Health Premium

The Ontario Health Premium need not have been such a political bomb-shell in our first year but for a campaign decision by Dalton and a few of his advisers. The leader felt he needed to assure voters that he wasn't just another tax-and-spend Liberal. So, three weeks before election day, on September 11, 2003, with many of our candidates standing behind him as backdrop (but *without* me), he signed a taxpayer protection pledge in a much-ballyhooed event with the Canadian Taxpayers Federation. Before a huge bank of television cameras, McGuinty assured Ontarians they could trust him to hold the line on taxes.

His television ads said it too. He looked into the camera, and with as much sincerity as he could muster he told people he wouldn't cut their taxes, but he wouldn't raise them either.

It was the one campaign commitment everyone would remember.

Shortly after this event, I approached Dalton with a simple question, premised on the assumption we were going to win the election. "What happens if soon after we win, the secretary to the Cabinet says, 'Premier, we have a $5 billion deficit? Which hospitals should we close? What programs should we cut to ensure we balance the budget — which you also promised to do?'"

His reply: "We'll deal with that problem if and when it arises."

It surely was an overly optimistic reply, since our finance critic, Gerry Phillips from Scarborough-Agincourt, had been warning Ontarians for months that the Ernie Eves government was probably hiding at least a $2 billion deficit. So we knew the state of the books wasn't good. We prayed that things might turn out better than we'd feared.

It was not to be the case. After the election, we appointed the departing provincial auditor, Erik Peters, to give us an auditor-like assessment of the province's finances. Even though we were only a little over halfway through the fiscal year, Peters told us the deficit was already at $5.6 billion. On the one hand, this was gold for us. We had a non-partisan, respected bureaucrat confirming our worst suspicions — that the Tories had been hiding a massive deficit. At a press conference following the release of Peters's report, I characterized what the report showed as "a stunning example of mismanagement and misrepresentation." The newspapers gave it great play in the next day's editions. It allowed us to send a message that throwing out the Tories was a very good decision by the electorate.

Of course, Peters's findings also presented us with an enormous conundrum. It was now clearly impossible for us to reconcile the three main financial commitments we had made during the 2003 election campaign: to balance the budget, to rebuild public services, and to do both without raising taxes.

The corporate tax increase in the Fall Economic Statement was not controversial, as we had made it one of our campaign proposals. Killing the private school tax credit proved to be somewhat more "involved." Again, we had campaigned on the elimination of the credit, but I had always assumed we would be doing it going forward. The premier and his advisers wanted it to be retroactive — effectively recapturing credits that parents were already counting on. It was a battle that I eventually lost. Apparently the premier wanted to make it very clear that public education, not private schools, was our priority.

With the economic statement complete, we turned our attention to the broad outlines of our first budget due the following spring. The question that animated our discussions in the ministry was how to accommodate our campaign commitments and yet not raise taxes. Many of my Cabinet colleagues began to press their cases. Gerard Kennedy, who had lost the 1996 Liberal leadership to Dalton McGuinty, was now education minister. He came to my home on a Sunday morning, pleading that we not retreat on our promises to rebuild public education.

"We can't afford politically to abandon the track we're on," he told me.

George Smitherman, the new health minister, made similar entreaties. Between the two of them, they controlled nearly two-thirds of all provincial spending. They were both aggressive and effective in trying to secure adequate resources for their priorities. They also frequently admonished the premier: "Don't let Sorbara derail our agenda. This is what we campaigned on!" I listened but made no commitments.

We engaged the public in our conundrum by launching extensive consultations in the Fall Economic Statement. We wanted input on whether we should abandon our spending plans but hold the line on taxes, or keep our campaign commitments but renege on the most high-profile commitment, not to raise taxes. At the start of the process I didn't have a definitive view on the question. But as the consultations went on I began to lean toward raising more revenues so we could deliver on our commitment to improve public services. My thinking was, we can make these investments, and if the economy stays strong we can balance the budget down the road. The premier kept expressing his hope that we could do it all without raising taxes or running deficits indefinitely.

The fact is, the voting public cares a lot less about the size of the deficit than about whether the local emergency room is staffed or their kids' teachers are in school and not on strike. Politically, it would have been much easier to run deficits and blame our predecessors for leaving us a mess.

I certainly did not dismiss that option out of hand. But, to his credit, the premier did. He thought it would be irresponsible for the province to go deeper into debt in the face of our campaign commitment to have balanced budgets.

Thus, our challenge in the ministry was how we would raise the $2 to $3 billion we would need to fulfill our health and education spending promises.

The first proposal we took to the premier was a value added tax. The plan was to transform Ontario's retail sales tax into a VAT, much like the federal GST. The ministry's economists loved the idea. Economists always prefer higher consumption taxes over higher income taxes because, they argue, higher income taxes put a damper on the incentive to work harder and earn more. I wasn't enamored with the VAT proposal but thought we should develop the idea and present it to the premier for his consideration. So we did.

With much fanfare we described the VAT plan to Premier McGuinty and his staff. It was summarily rejected. "Yeah, we're not going to do that," I remember Dalton saying. "We gotta find another way." The VAT fell flat.

However, someone in the premier's office, perhaps Gerald Butts, did give us a useful piece of advice, suggesting we come up with something more directly connected to the programs we wanted to implement. Given that we were looking to improve access and delivery of health care, why not create a revenue tool related directly to that plan? After days of analysis and debate we settled on the broad parameters of a new tax, to be called the Ontario Health Premium, with all revenues going directly to funding the new initiatives being developed by the health ministry.

We took the proposal to the premier and his senior staff. McGuinty always liked to start such meetings with a joke or a jab to put everyone in a relaxed mood. "Okay, Sorbara, what poison do you have for us today?" he quipped.

I led the presentation and then handed the technical details over to my officials. The premier chaired the ensuing discussion, canvassing the room and making sure everyone felt comfortable weighing in. He never allowed the atmosphere to get intimidating, where people felt they couldn't offer an opinion. In short order there was a consensus around the table that we had hit on an acceptable solution.

The Ontario Health Premium was to be a hybrid progressive tax administered through the income tax system, and levied on the basis of people's taxable income. The tax would raise the $2 billion we needed to fulfill our commitments and wouldn't be an enormous burden on individual taxpayers. We capped it at $900 for upper-income Ontarians. A full 44 percent of Ontarians wouldn't pay it at all, and we felt good about that. The average family would pay $250 a year, and every penny realized would go straight to health care. The discussion then turned to the politics of bringing in a new tax less than nine months after being elected on the promise of no new taxes. There were no easy answers. Certainly calling the tax a health premium helped explain why we were increasing taxes, but no one was naive enough to think that a huge political storm would not blow in the moment I read our first budget.

The premier summed up what we were in for. "We are going to get beat up very badly," he said. "But we have to do this. It's the right thing to do. It would be far worse to turn our backs on the things we need to do in health and education."

All of the people around that table except me were new to government. All of us were still basking in the honeymoon phase of a successful election. And none of us, including me, were really prepared for the rage that would sweep the province — fanned by both the opposition parties — as soon as the premium was announced.

We decided then and there to do all we could to prepare for the worst, including a communications strategy that made no attempt to sugar-coat our decision.

Thus, in the opening section of my first budget speech, on May 18, 2004, I said:

Mr. Speaker, every budget is about choices. We have made two important choices that are especially difficult — to increase revenues and to balance the budget over a number of years. They are choices that are inconsistent with our election commitments. We openly acknowledge that. However, it would simply not be possible to deliver a balanced budget this year without destabilizing vital public services and perhaps even the economy itself. Such an approach would be irresponsible and we reject it.

Noble words, perhaps, but to no avail. The storm broke even before I had completed my budget speech. No sooner had I referred to the new tax than a constant chorus of catcalls erupted from the opposition benches, interrupting the balance of my remarks. They were led by John Baird, the Tory finance critic, who was so loud and offensive that he was eventually ejected from the legislature for the remainder of the day.

It got worse. Over the next several days virtually all of our members took a tongue lashing from constituents who were angry, or disappointed, or both. It was certainly hardest on the premier who, after all, had made the high-profile "no new taxes" pledge. He was called a liar and we were tagged with the "Fiberals" label. Although the premier never uttered a word of complaint to me, I could sense that a lot of people in his office were angry at me because their boss was getting beaten up so badly.

For the most part I took the storm in stride, perhaps because I had been through some similar wars during the Peterson years, but most especially because I remained very proud of the budget and the positive course it had set for a province in desperate need of better public services.

To make matters worse, the Ontario Health Premium drew anger from our federal cousins, the Liberal Party of Canada, who were set for a federal general election on June 28, just weeks after my budget. Our members and our party heard repeatedly from federal Liberal candidates in Ontario who were getting an earful as they went door to door. I was not surprised. When voters are angry they tend to vent without discrimination when a candidate comes knocking. Now federal Liberal candidates were being called into account for a budget they had nothing to do with.

The result of the national election was a heavy blow to the federal

Liberals, and in retrospect the beginning of the end for their time in government. Prime Minister Paul Martin lost the majority he inherited and had to settle for a minority government. That minority would later be succeeded by Stephen Harper's first minority government. Many suggested — but I, for one, never accepted — that the Ontario Health Premium contributed significantly to the federal Liberals' fall from grace. Yes, they lost twenty-five seats in Ontario. But they also lost fifteen seats in Quebec and two in Manitoba, and there was no new health premium in those provinces. The fact is, we could not have shaped our budget to satisfy the political and electoral needs of another party in another jurisdiction. We simply did what we had to do.

In the end, we expected all that was being thrown at us. But there was also the law of unintended consequences, which we hadn't considered. Back in the old days, Ontario Health Insurance Plan (OHIP) premiums used to be a benefit that employers and employees bargained over. In almost all cases, employers agreed to pay the premiums of their salaried employees, particularly in workplaces where contracts were collectively bargained. Of course, when the premium disappeared under former Liberal treasurer Robert Nixon in the late 1980s, so did the obligation of employers to pay on behalf of their employees. Now, however, many unions were saying, "If this is a premium, then our employers should pay it, because collective agreements require employers to pay for any provincial health premium." My officials were adamant that, the name notwithstanding, it really wasn't a premium, but the unions didn't care. They took many employers to arbitration and onward to divisional court, to try to shift the burden of the Ontario Health Premium to their employers. In most cases the courts held that the Ontario Health Premium was not the resurrection of the long-forgotten OHIP premium; but for a while a number of large unionized employers wondered whether we had lost our senses.

We also did one other thing in that 2004 budget that turned out to be politically damaging, although none of us saw it coming. To show how tough we intended to be on spending — even on health-care spending — we de-listed some chiropractic and optometry services. In other words, we told people who used those services that the province would no longer pay the bills. If people wanted those services they had to pay for them themselves. By doing this, we invited the question, "How can you be charging us more for health care, but delivering less?" It was good public policy to de-list those services. But it was a devastating political move that caused yet more angst for our caucus.

In hindsight, we didn't need to do it. It caused us unnecessary headaches and ultimately didn't save that much money.

The full force of the Ontario Health Premium storm did subside eventually, even if it left permanent scars on our reputation and lasting fodder for the opposition parties for the next election. In time most people came to realize that the premium was improving both access to and the quality of care in Ontario. Moreover, the many other initiatives in Budget 2004 were making a difference — peace in our schools, new money for transit, and the creation of the Greenbelt around Toronto, to name a few.

Today, the Ontario Health Premium survives. It's raising $3 billion a year. And every penny goes to health care. It remains one small box on every Ontarian's income tax form. It's line 260. In my view it's been an enduring example of doing what is necessary to strengthen public services. And despite the political outcries, no party has ever promised to repeal the health premium in the three subsequent elections. I'll take that any day.

The York Subway Saga

November 27, 2009, was a really good day.

On that day a ground-breaking ceremony launched the construction of the subway extension to York University and northward into the heart of Vaughan.

The mayor of Toronto, David Miller, called it an unprecedented example of co-operation among four levels of government. For me, it was the realization of a dream that had started more than a quarter of a century before, with a very casual conversation with my seatmate in the Ontario legislature.

It was 1986. I was a rookie MPP and the minister for colleges and universities in Premier David Peterson's minority government. Sitting next to me in the legislature was Ed Fulton, the MPP for Scarborough East and minister of transportation.

"Ed," I said, "take out your map." Ed always carried a map of the city of Toronto and its transit system with him. He laid it out on his desk. "Let me show you the next piece of subway in Toronto that you should promote," I said.

I took out my pen and drew a line from the Wilson Station — at the northernmost end of the University-Spadina subway line — to York University, which occupied more than 450 acres of land in Toronto's northwest end, right on the boundary with York Region to the north.

Ed looked at me and simply said: "You've gotta be crazy."

When you get that kind of reaction from the minister of transportation, it's kind of a conversation stopper. But the next day in the legislature, Ed continued the conversation.

"I've talked to my bureaucrats about your idea, and they don't think you're completely crazy."

That was music to my ears. It was a tangible sign that the idea of extending the subway to where the population of the GTA — the Greater Toronto Area — was growing significantly was not just a personal fantasy.

I've been in love with subways since, at eighteen years old, I took my first trip to London, England. I was enthralled with the Tube. Fast forward two decades and I'm now an elected politician with a dream. I thought the idea of a subway linking the two biggest universities in Ontario, the University of Toronto and York University, made real sense. I imagined a burgeoning relationship between the two campuses, where students could take courses at each one and be linked with a modern, sleek form of transit. It felt like the logical thing to do.

I will also admit that if I could bring a subway to York's Keele Street campus — the southern boundary of York Region and my riding — it would not only be great for the people in the region, but also for my political prospects.

Very little happened after that conversation with Ed Fulton — at least nothing on the subway idea.

Two years later, however, with a huge parliamentary majority and the possibility of an early election, the Peterson government determined that public transit was a hot item and a visionary transit plan was in order. It was called Let's Move, and its centrepiece was the "looping" of the Yonge-University-Spadina subway lines. Instead of having the subway stop at a dead end at the Wilson Station in the northwest, or the Finch Station at the top of the Yonge line, Let's Move advocated extending the University--Spadina line to York University and then east under Steeles Avenue to join the Yonge line, extending it, as well, to Steeles Avenue. Experts agreed that moving people in a constant loop would be more efficient than the present system with its dead ends. There was huge community support for Let's Move. A group in York Region called the Loop Group, led by local politicians such as Mario Racco, a Vaughan councillor, became devoted champions.

Let's Move formed part of the Liberal platform in the September 1990 election. Then disaster struck.

On election night, September 6, 1990, while I recaptured my York Centre seat, other Liberals were going down in flames around Ontario. We lost fifty-nine seats, including Premier David Peterson's in London Centre. And we lost the government to Bob Rae's New Democrats.

Priorities change when governments change. Suddenly the subway extension to York University was on the back burner. Suddenly the top priority was a subway under Eglinton Avenue West to Black Creek Drive, the heart of Premier Rae's York South riding. Frankly, I never thought there was the population growth or economic activity to justify building an Eglinton line rather than the York University extension. But that was Rae's call, he was entitled to make it, and he did.

Over the next decade and beyond the politics of transit in Toronto can best be described as a comedy of errors. Rae's government began to build the Eglinton West line, and then the Harris government, never big supporters of public transit, killed the Eglinton line and provided the Toronto Transit Commission (TTC) with funds to build the Sheppard East line as a favour to Mayor Mel Lastman. From the day the ribbon was cut, the Sheppard line has been a grossly underutilized money-losing proposition.

Things changed when Dalton McGuinty won the 2003 election and I became his minister of finance. It occurred to me that I might finally be in a position to reopen the discussion on a subway to York. The premier and his Cabinet agreed that we needed to do a lot more on urban infrastructure in Toronto, and that included public transit. I once again argued that the first priority ought to be a subway extension to York University.

As a practical matter, being minister of finance responsible for a $100-billion annual budget wasn't enough to make the subway extension a reality. First of all, it's actually the TTC that has the responsibility to make decisions on subway extensions. And the TTC takes direction from its political master, Toronto City Council and its mayor, who at the time was David Miller. When I talked to Miller about York, he was less than enthusiastic. Scarborough was a higher priority for him. But my mission was to get people on board for the York extension. So I talked to the politicians in Vaughan who I knew would get behind it. I lobbied my Cabinet and caucus colleagues, and in particular MPPs from north Toronto and Peel and York Regions. I talked to ministry of transportation officials to urge their support. I included references to a York University subway in speeches whenever it was appropriate. And I tried to get Toronto municipal politicians to list it as one of their top priorities. A great deal of work was done by people associated with York University, including Seymour Schulich, who personally funded one of the studies that supported the case for the subway. A strong coalition was emerging.

Then came a strange twist. In late 2005, caught up in an RCMP investigation, I had to resign from the finance portfolio. While all of us in caucus knew that the theme of Budget 2006 would be infrastructure investment, I was out of the loop as far as the specific details went. Dwight Duncan was now in charge.

On budget day, March 23, 2006, Duncan announced that the government would extend the Spadina subway line not just to York University but to Vaughan City Centre. I was blown away. Ironically, people referred to it as "the Sorbara Subway" because of my efforts over the years to make it happen. But I was as surprised as the next guy when funding was allocated in the budget for the project. I actually had no involvement in the developing storyline.

How serious was the McGuinty government about getting this subway extension built? As it turns out, plenty. By the spring of 2006, tax revenues were far more buoyant than the ministry had anticipated. So instead of a budgetary commitment to flow the money at some indeterminate point in the future, Duncan actually set aside $670 million for the York extension, along with additional money for Brampton's and Mississauga's transit needs. He put the money into a special-purpose trust account. That was highly unusual — but it showed how serious we were about bringing this project to fruition. It was the government's way of saying, "This money is for the York extension and we're setting it aside in this special account — and don't anyone even think for a second about spending it on anything else."

That was the financial side of things. Politically, the government was taking a high-stakes risk by funding the project in this way. After all, we didn't yet have the support of any of the municipalities with whom we would be partnering.

We had no assurance from the Toronto Transit Commission, or the city of Toronto, or the city of Vaughan, or York Region that they'd pay to play. The budget made clear that for this to happen, they'd all have to contribute. I had to hand it to Dwight — that was pretty impressive risk-taking and leadership.

York Region immediately signed on. Incredibly, David Miller was still cool to the idea. He should have been thrilled at the prospect of the province providing $670 million for more subway infrastructure, regardless of where it went. The politics of competing priorities in transit can be confounding for Toronto's mayor. And a municipal election was not too far off.

Moreover, we were proposing something that had never been done before. We were asking Toronto's transit authority to help pay for an expansion of its subway system beyond the borders of the city. So I wasn't surprised that some grumbled, asking why local taxpayers in Toronto should pay to extend a subway to Vaughan.

The day after Victoria Day 2006, I returned to Cabinet as minister of finance and took over responsibility for the subway initiative, including getting the federal government to buy in. Dwight Duncan's transit plan called for contributions from the federal government as well as the city of Toronto and York Region. We needed Stephen Harper's government to become a partner with us.

I had raised the issue of the York extension with my federal counterpart Jim Flaherty numerous times. Flaherty and I knew each other well. We sat together at Queen's Park from 2001 until 2005, when he resigned his provincial seat to run for Stephen Harper's Conservative Party, becoming Harper's new finance minister after the January 2006 federal election. When I returned to finance in May, Jim and I quickly developed a good working relationship. We were political adversaries no doubt, but without the venom that sometimes infects the world of politics. Whenever I'd talk to Flaherty I would remind him that federal participation was essential to the York subway mission, and that it would be good politics for his government and for him personally, given that he was the political minister for the Greater Toronto Area.

At first, Flaherty was a skeptic. He reminded me that subways were very expensive to build. My mission was to continue to try to win him over.

Meanwhile, we still needed the TTC and the city of Toronto to sign on, and they were moving oh so slowly. Mayor Miller finally came on board, albeit reluctantly. Howard Moscoe, a North York city councillor who was chair of the TTC, argued that I had a conflict of interest in pursuing the York extension because my family's business, The Sorbara Group, owned apartment buildings on Keele Street, a couple of kilometres away from the project. I thought Howard's objections were little more than political grandstanding, and I guess the TTC did too, because eventually it, too, supported the York line.

But there was still Jim Flaherty. I needed an opportunity to put the case directly to him. I saw one on the horizon: in December 2006, the federal and provincial finance ministers were to meet in Vancouver. I phoned Flaherty before the meeting and I said to him, "Jim, I need ten minutes alone with you in Vancouver." He agreed to meet.

And yet, when the Vancouver meetings came to an end, I saw him and his entourage, bags in hand, heading for the exit. *Wait!* I thought. *What about my meeting?*

I ran over to him. "Jim, we need to talk." We stepped into a nearby private room. "Jim, you have to be in this project," I told him. "We need you to support it." I made the financial and political arguments yet again. And then it was time to barter.

Flaherty said he needed a commitment from me to extend Highway 407 east and widen Highway 7 east of Brock Road to Whitby and Oshawa. He was the MP for Whitby-Oshawa, and these road improvements were provincial responsibilities.

I was quick to respond: "No problem. The congestion there is as bad as anywhere. The 407 is my number-one highway priority. I'll get this done for you." It would cost $1.5 billion to make these improvements, but the 407 is a toll highway, meaning that over time the province would realize significant revenues, and the improvements would eventually pay for themselves.

We shook hands. We had a meeting of minds.

But just because two finance ministers shake hands on an agreement doesn't mean it's a done deal. Flaherty would also have to get approval on his end. I had sufficient respect for his clout in Ottawa that I felt he'd get it done. Then I found myself calling him every few weeks just to check in and see how things were proceeding. It was taking a long time. He kept saying, "Greg, there's some stuff I've gotta work through." I realized he had his own issues to deal with at Treasury Board and the prime minister's office. But I also knew the federal Conservatives were looking to win more seats in the GTA, and this would help in that area.

Eventually Flaherty came through. He pledged $660 million as the federal portion of our transit plan. All that was left was to craft a communication plan.

At the outset I imagined an announcement where Jim and I would share the podium, demonstrating some rare federal–provincial harmony. But the announcement became so important to both governments that Prime Minister Harper's and Premier McGuinty's offices took it over. That was fine with me. I didn't care who'd be standing in the strongest beam of the spotlight.

Despite a long history of animosity between the Harper and McGuinty governments, the March 2007 announcement at Downsview Park went off without a hitch. (Well, almost without a hitch. We started late because the prime minister's motorcade was caught in traffic.) Jim and I shared the stage with the prime minister and the premier. After the political fanfare was over, the real work began: more than two years of difficult negotiations among four levels of government, agencies such as the TTC, Metrolinx (Ontario's regional transit planning body), York University, community groups, architects, engineers, and, of course, private landowners under whose lands the subway would pass. What was required and what was ultimately achieved was an unprecedented level of co-operation and compromise among all the players at the table. A measure of that complexity is the fact that the subway's construction did not begin until four years after the deal with Jim Flaherty was inked.

This "done deal" nearly came off the rails after the 2007 election. The then Ontario transportation minister, Kathleen Wynne, decided to divide in half the commitment I'd made to Flaherty. She wanted to extend the 407 only to Simcoe Street in Oshawa, even though I'd promised the full extension to Highways 35/115 near Port Hope.

When Flaherty heard about this, he hit the roof. He felt betrayed. "This breaches the commitment made by the provincial government," he told our officials and the media.

I was no longer finance minister, but I did confirm to our people that my commitment was for the whole thing. Yes, Flaherty and I did the deal with a handshake. No, there were no notes or signed documents. But I'd given my word.

I tried to assuage Flaherty by assuring him the full extension of Highway 407 would happen, that this was just the first phase and a second would follow. That seemed to mollify him.

So my dream for a York University subway extension is actually happening. The 8.6-kilometre extension should be ready for the travelling public by 2016. It constitutes the longest extension to the subway network in almost four decades. It'll carry hundreds of thousands of passengers each year. It'll connect with York Region's VIVA bus service and a potential GO Transit service along the 407. It'll kick start development of a fabulous new Vaughan Metropolitan Centre. It'll take sixteen hundred bus trips a day *off* the road and thousands more car trips to York University, easing traffic congestion. York University is now a sea of parking lots and diesel buses. That can't and shouldn't continue. The University-Spadina portion of the subway line will now get more use, making it more valuable and efficient. And it'll put York University at the centre of a new Greater Toronto Area. Yes, it'll cost $2 billion, but I have no doubt that every single penny will be worth it. Congestion is the number-one issue in the GTA. Unless you're prepared to prohibit more people or cars from coming to Toronto, these are the things you have to do to transform people's lives.

Certainly, I championed the subway in part because it helped the part of the province I represented in the Ontario legislature. I don't apologize for that. It's an essential ingredient in the recipe. Every project that goes forward has to have strong merit in and of itself. But that's not enough. In our system, you need unrelenting political advocacy to win your case. The job of the politician is to make that case. Would this project have happened had I not been there? That is difficult to answer. There are limited resources and all kinds of players competing to put those resources to work somewhere. And, you need good luck as well. I often wonder whether, if Jim Flaherty had escaped from Vancouver without my seeing him before he reached the exit, we would still just be imagining a subway extension to York. I'm just glad he didn't stand me up because a plane was waiting.

My work on a York subway started in 1986. It will open in 2016. That's thirty years. But I'm glad to say, the job is almost done.

However, I am truly saddened that the man who contributed the final piece to the puzzle will not be there to ride the first train through York University to the Vaughan Metropolitan Centre. Three weeks after stepping down as federal finance minister in March 2014, Jim Flaherty died of a massive heart attack at his apartment in Ottawa. He gave his life to serving his country in the best way he could, and he paid a heavy price.

Jim Flaherty will be remembered as one of Canada's most influential finance ministers and one of its most animated political actors. Through his years in finance I had serious reservations about some of the policies he pursued. Reducing the GST from 7 to 5 percent, for example, was clearly bad fiscal policy, even if it was good Conservative politics.

But I never doubted his commitment to his work and the passion and integrity with which he pursued it. Canadians will surely miss him.

The Ontario Child Benefit

There was considerable drama surrounding the budget of spring 2007. Some of it the public knew about. Some of it only I knew about.

Everyone knew that, by law, this would be our last budget before the 2007 election. Despite the fanfare around Throne Speeches, it is now the annual budget that has become the planning document for all modern governments, including Ontario. A pre-election budget inevitably sets the stage for the campaign that follows. Thus, I was keenly aware of how important it was to get it right. As confident as I was that we were on the right track, I knew Budget 2007 might also be my last chance to have a meaningful policy impact on the province's future. I also knew this would be our government's last and most significant chance to set the tone for a successful fall campaign on October 10, 2007. Everybody knew all of the above.

What people didn't know — not the public, not the Cabinet, not the caucus, not even the premier — was that I had made a commitment to my wife Kate to make Budget 2007 my last. Our plan was that after the 2007 election I would forgo the workload that came with being minister of finance.

By the spring of 2007, Ontario's economic prospects were uniformly positive and the province's treasury was in very good shape. Although we had inherited a $5.6 billion deficit in 2003, the sunshine had now returned to Ontario's finances. This would be our government's fourth budget (my third), and I was feeling much more on top of the work. More important, as chair of the 2007 re-election campaign, I knew Budget 2007 would frame much of the upcoming general election. I wanted it to be a home run. From our first days in government we had decided that each budget would have an overarching theme. The political calculus for Budget 2007 was quite simple. We would be able to satisfy those on the right of the political spectrum with a budget that was balanced. Some in our caucus even advocated for tax cuts, given how buoyant the economy was, and how much we'd raised taxes in our first budget in 2004. But it didn't feel as if there was much untapped support on our right flank, so we rejected those ideas.

On the other hand there was a huge swath of Ontarians who had not really felt sufficient tangible benefit from our first three years in power. We soon settled on a theme: to address the needs of vulnerable populations who, more than the average middle class family, look to government to aid them in their journeys. In political terms we determined that Budget 2007 would lean decidedly to the left. Our hope was that in the ensuing election campaign, left-leaning voters would see McGuinty Liberals as a good bet for the next four years.

It is axiomatic that inside the finance ministry, officials argue persistently for restraint. Typically, they take the position, with supporting statistics, that there's just not enough money for new programs. It is a culture deeply rooted in saying no. I had come to understand that such an approach was a matter of professional responsibility. What I learned is that sometimes you have to take those warnings with a grain of salt. Thus far in finance my experience was that the economy continued to outperform forecasts; our revenues were higher than anticipated, as were our savings.

Two years prior to Budget 2007, seminal work began in Ontario on the issue of child poverty. A coalition known as the Campaign Against Child Poverty had been formed, with leadership that read like a who's who of experts in the field. One of its leaders, Laurel Rothman, was particularly effective in building the case for support and in creating a bridge to government and political policy-makers. Having decided we wanted to do something historic for vulnerable people, we had frequent meetings with a variety of poverty groups and the premier's office staff. Work was going on within government as well. The premier had appointed Deb Matthews and Kathleen Wynne as co-chairs of the Cabinet Committee on Poverty Reduction.

This work resulted in a proposal to create a new support program directed specifically at improving the plight of children living in or close to poverty. It was to become known as the Ontario Child Benefit. The advocates ultimately convinced us to make the Ontario Child Benefit the centrepiece of our final budget. I became smitten with the idea. The name itself succinctly described what we wanted this new program to be: support for vulnerable children in Ontario. We were convinced the Ontario Child Benefit could have a discernible long-term impact on children living in poverty. And for a *Liberal* finance minister, doing this kind of good is an opportunity that comes along only rarely. We needed to seize the moment.

Our research indicated the Ontario Child Benefit would help nearly 1.3 million children. Over five years, it would put more than $2 billion into lifting up vulnerable children. Low-income parents would be encouraged to move off welfare, knowing they didn't have to risk losing support for their kids. The state of the treasury dictated that we start modestly — just $250 per child per year — but with increases in each succeeding year, it would ramp up to $1,100 per child in four years.

Many people inside and outside of government contributed to the creation of the Ontario Child Benefit. But there is one fellow in particular, Dr. Charles Pascal — Chuck, to his friends — whose fingerprints were all over the program's successful birth. Chuck has been a dear friend and adviser to me for thirty years. He has a long history of public service, everything from being a former deputy minister of education to president of Sir Sandford Fleming College in Peterborough. At this time, however, he was executive director of the Atkinson Foundation, which promotes social justice. Chuck, ably assisted by his protégé Pedro Barata, played a crucial role as the liaison between poverty groups and my ministry. He pushed us in the ministry to make the Ontario Child Benefit a reality, and then to increase the generosity of the program. But he also pushed the coalition to be reasonable, arguing that a modest but solidly established program designed to grow over time was the best way to go, and not to let the perfect become the enemy of the good.

Obviously, there was a good deal of political debate as to how the Ontario Child Benefit and the other social justice initiatives in Budget 2007 would play politically. Some were entirely skeptical about the campaign value of the budget's main themes. Others, like Don Guy, our party's public opinion guru and campaign director, offered an informed caution based on reliable polling data.

"Every time you mention the words 'vulnerable Ontarians,' our numbers go down," he told me. Don wasn't arguing against the direction we were proposing. On the contrary, he led the way in shaping our communications from the outset. But he was saying there's a big chunk of the Ontario public that wonders why we're spending their tax dollars on poor people who don't vote anyway. True enough: the Ontario Child Benefit was not about buying the votes of the recipients; rather, it was about doing something important that truly reflected the values that our caucus, our Cabinet, and our party held dear.

"Our responsibility is to ensure that this new economic strength improves the lives of our people," I said in the budget speech in the legislature. "We continue that mission with new resources for Ontario's children."

It was one of my proudest moments in public life.

The reaction to the budget was heartwarming. The stakeholders were thrilled. We received notes, phone calls, and feedback that were uniformly supportive and grateful.

What a difference, I thought at the time, between this budget and my first, between the Ontario Health Premium and the Ontario Child Benefit. The health premium represented a broken promise, and only happened after several fits and starts in the talks between the premier's office and the ministry of finance. We were then a young and inexperienced government. Conversely, the Ontario Child Benefit exemplified the finest in small "l" liberal policy, and was the result of excellent, experienced collaboration between the premier's office, my ministry, and a public advocacy coalition that was constructive, rather than combative.

Budget 2007 was, in my view, one of Ontario's best, if the criterion is helping people who need it most. I'm proud of the Ontario Child Benefit. All these years later, it's still there helping poor kids.

It was great policy, but it was also great politics, as it positioned us well for a bruising re-election campaign that would help Dalton McGuinty make history.

7

Cleared! A Return to Cabinet

During my hiatus from electoral politics from 1995 to 2001, I really wasn't in the market for positions on boards of directors in the way that some ex-politicians are. Two interests were driving my professional life. First, I wanted to make the St. Catharines Stompers baseball team a success. And second, I wanted to bring some of The Sorbara Group expertise in land development to the newly liberated Czechoslovakia.

But there was one local company in York Region that I did find intriguing. One day in 1993 when I was still an opposition MPP, I got a call from a businessman named Vic De Zen. He wanted me, as his local MPP, to come up to his factory in Woodbridge to see what he was building. Vic De Zen was the principal shareholder of Royal Plastics Limited. Over the previous decade, Royal had become one of Canada's largest producers of plastic components, from window frames to PVC pipes to vinyl window covering. Now he was developing a revolutionary new way to build ultra-low-cost homes based on plastic extrusion columns, linked together Lego-style and then filled after assembly with concrete. The business plan was to market the Royal Building System in countries desperate for low-cost housing in the form of extra-sturdy thousand-square-foot homes costing a few thousand dollars. While I didn't know Vic well, the Canadian business community did. He was a successful and brilliant entrepreneur who had been featured on the covers of magazines and was winning awards for the excellence of his products and the impressive growth of his business.

A year later, buoyed by the potential for the Royal Building System and in need of growth capital, Royal decided to become a public company. The initial public offering (IPO) was developed with the aid of the Bank of Nova Scotia, and in November 1994 Royal's shares began trading on the Toronto Stock Exchange.

Part of the process of becoming a public company is the appointment of outside directors to the company's board. Their primary responsibilities include a special obligation to represent the interests of the outside shareholders of the corporation.

Vic invited me, along with three others, to join Royal's board as outside directors.

Fascinated by the growth potential for Royal's new technologies, and feeling that I could apply my legal and governance experience to the growth of a public company, I accepted the appointment. At our board's first meeting I was made chair of the Royal audit committee.

The terms of the Royal IPO were standard fare at that time for new public companies created and grown by the entrepreneurship and savvy of a sole proprietor. The IPO gave most of the power to manage the company to the former proprietor — in this case, Vic De Zen.

Vic was to be granted multiple voting shares with twenty times the voting rights of other shareholders. He was to serve as both the CEO and chair of the board; inside directors controlled the business of the board. The IPO also provided that only transactions involving more than $60 million need be taken to the board for approval.

The overall message to the market was that the ongoing success of Royal depended on the ability of the founder and his team to continue to control all aspects of the company's operation.

The first five years of Royal's life as a public company were dominated by rapid growth. Annual profits were strong, and hundreds of millions were spent each year on new plant facilities and the acquisition of small companies that meshed well with Royal's expanding reach. The company's name was changed to Royal Group Technologies Limited to reflect the new emphasis on the science behind the growth.

At the same time, however, the world of corporate governance was changing dramatically. Expansion of shareholder rights and the curtailment of executives' authority were on the agenda in every boardroom on the continent. In the United States, the federal Sarbanes-Oxley Act drove the transformation of corporate governance. In Ontario, the Ontario Securities Commission (OSC) was setting new standards.

Multiple voting shares were no longer in vogue. The roles of board chair and CEO were to be separated. Outside directors were to have the majority voice on boards, and audit committees were to have only outside directors on them.

Royal, and in particular Vic De Zen, had no appetite for the governance changes that were becoming the new standard. It was a shortcoming that was to have grave consequences for Vic, for his senior executives, and for me.

By 2000, storm clouds were threatening Royal from a number of directions. Our governing structure was increasingly out of step. The company was beginning to feel the hangover from growth that was too rapid; competition, especially from China, was eating into revenues; net profits were down, and shareholders were anxious to find out whether Royal would ever pay a corporate dividend.

In six years, Royal had gone from being the poster child for Canadian entrepreneurship to a "troubled adolescent" company.

As I took up my responsibilities in the ministry of finance, I could not have imagined that my time with Royal would harm me or the new McGuinty administration. On the contrary, it stood to reason that my years on the board of an Ontario-based global public company would add to the experience needed to understand the demands of overseeing Ontario's economic affairs.

In that regard I was deeply mistaken.

Late in 2003, the Ontario Securities Commission began a confidential investigation of some aspects of Royal's business practices. Despite the confidential nature of the probe, the OSC's chairman, David Brown, notified staff in the ministry of finance of the investigation. Word about it was passed on to me. This put me in a classic "Catch 22" situation.

I had sat on Royal's board, and as minister of finance I had governmental responsibility for the OSC. Because the investigation was confidential I was bound not to disclose the matter to anyone. It was Royal's responsibility to disclose the investigation to the public in accordance with the ongoing disclosure rules for all public companies. But Royal remained silent.

Three months later, on February 24, 2004, the RCMP, the OSC, and federal tax authorities finally announced a far-reaching investigation of Royal.

Immediately there were calls from the opposition parties for my resignation. These only intensified when I acknowledged I had been advised of the investigation in December. Smelling blood, they were not satisfied by my assertion that the law did not permit me to disclose the fact of the investigation to anyone so long as it remained a confidential matter.

Dalton and I met urgently. I assured him that I knew absolutely nothing about the substance of the investigation other than that I had been advised about it confidentially in December, for reasons I still did not understand. Out of an abundance of caution we agreed to transfer responsibility for the OSC to Gerry Phillips, at that time our chair of the management board of Cabinet. While that was the right thing to do, it certainly did not satisfy the thirst of the opposition. Through the balance of the year and into the next, as each new revelation appeared about the investigation, there were renewed cries for my head. Repeated applications landed on the desk of the province's Integrity Commissioner, Justice Coulter Osborne, to declare that Ontario's finance minister was in an open conflict of interest. In each case the commissioner rejected the allegations. He went so far as to assert that it was somewhat inappropriate for the OSC to advise me of a confidential investigation.

At that point I thought that the matter was closed. Except that it wasn't.

In an effort to crack down on white-collar crime in Canada, the federal government had created IMET — the Integrated Market Enforcement Team. The feds put a lot of money into IMET and decided Royal Group Technologies would be one of its first targets. Politically, Royal was easy prey. It was run by an Italian-Canadian entrepreneur who wasn't a big fan of the new business realities for public companies. And rumours spread that Vic was diverting Royal's money to prop up a Marriott resort development on the West Indies island of St. Kitts. The rumours were false, as the RCMP investigators discovered after their auditors descended on Royal's offices.

But IMET was determined to find something. After months of investigation, the team settled on allegations that Vic had a conflict of interest in some of his business dealings with Royal. There were two separate parts to the story.

Vic had purchased a large swath of land for development in Woodbridge, north of Toronto. Shortly after the purchase he sold that land to Royal for a modest profit. IMET said he should have sold it to Royal at what he paid for it.

The second allegation related to the sale of one of Royal Group's subsidiaries. The purchaser issued a number of warrants to Royal as part of the consideration in the deal. The warrants were held by Royal for a year. Then Royal's senior management allocated the warrants to a few senior executives as part of an annual bonus for them. IMET insisted those warrants should have stayed with the company.

In keeping with the theme of their case, IMET's people searched for further instances of conflict of interest. They finally found something that involved me. This made for great copy for the RCMP. They had in their crosshairs not just a rich Italian-Canadian entrepreneur but also a high-profile Italian-Canadian politician. The story was suddenly front page news.

A forensic audit on Royal revealed that in the late 1990s, Royal bought a small building from The Sorbara Group for $2 million. Because I had an indirect interest in the company that owned the building, IMET alleged that I should have revealed that indirect interest to the board at the time of the sale. Failure to do so, they argued, constituted a conflict of interest. This became Alice in Wonderland stuff. I had never seen or heard of the building that was the subject of the conflict allegation; nor did I know that The Sorbara Group had sold it to Royal. How then was I supposed to declare a conflict of interest to Royal's board? Again, no transactions worth less than $60 million came before the board for consideration. No one on the board was ever informed about the purchase or that the building had been owned by a Sorbara Group company. But IMET was desperate to link me to the larger case against Royal's senior management. On October 11, 2005, investigators raided The Sorbara Group's offices, hoping to find evidence to nail me to the wall. Two RCMP officers sat in The Sorbara Group lobby, refusing to allow anyone to enter or leave the premises. Long-time Sorbara Group staffer Janice Martin was tasked with the job of walking the RCMP through the offices. She tried to tell the Mounties that "Greg wouldn't know a Sorbara Group building if he tripped over one," but they weren't interested.

Janice's statement, while cryptic, was absolutely true. Some forty years ago my father had reorganized The Sorbara Group so that each of his four children would hold an equal share of the business as it grew. For that purpose he used a series of holding companies and trusts. But neither my sister nor I had ever actually worked in the businesses, and neither of us knew much about the hundreds of industrial buildings that made up The Sorbara Group portfolio of real estate. That was left to my brothers Joseph and Edward, who ran the businesses over the years, and did it very well. Indeed, friends used to chide me about the fact that my role at The Sorbara Group was to cash dividend cheques — which, though humbling, was true.

As for Royal, had its senior management been somewhat more diligent, they might have advised me that they were purchasing an industrial building from The Sorbara Group so as to permit time to note a conflict of interest at a subsequent board meeting. Regrettably, that never happened.

In the Introduction to this book, I described the hours after the RCMP raid. By 9:30 that evening I had resigned as minister of finance. For a day or so I was simply in shock. The search warrants were sealed, so I had no information whatsoever as to why I was being investigated. Indeed, it took some weeks before I was told about the allegation of conflict relating to the purchase of an industrial building by Royal. What preoccupied me at the outset was what I would have to do to convince the RCMP that they had made a serious mistake. I worried that I could never regain my reputation; the notion of ever returning as minister of finance was speculative at best.

The first order of business was to put together a strong legal team. It included

- Julian Porter, the country's best libel lawyer, because I believed I had a case for defamation against the national police force;
- Frank Marrocco from the Gowlings law firm, whom I had known for years, to handle the criminal defence;

- Glenn Hainey and Lynn Mahoney, who took over for Frank when he was appointed a judge of the Ontario Supreme Court;
- Rod McLeod, a former Ontario deputy attorney general, whose expertise as an intermediary with the RCMP could have put a stop to the case before a court hearing; and
- Jim Riley, an old friend from my Stikeman Elliott days and a lawyer who had done significant work for Royal. Though he was not directly part of the team, Jim's one phone call to me saved me a fortune in legal fees. He simply advised that Royal, through its insurance for board members, should be responsible for all my legal fees.

From day one, the real challenge was managing my emotions. The humiliation of such a public "hanging" is not inconsequential. I was gripped by anger, embarrassment, and helplessness in equal measure. I could almost hear the whispers about yet another politician — this time an Italian Canadian, to boot — falling from grace.

I quickly learned not to let those emotions and fears overcome me. I knew that I had done nothing wrong, that the RCMP had made a terrible mistake in its determination to bring down Vic De Zen, and even if the rest of the world never learned the truth I was satisfied that I knew the truth and that was all that mattered. Soon I realized that I could live a very fulfilling life, even if I was never again a very important person in a very important government. Even more important was that my wife, Kate, and I suddenly had far more personal time together. While I continued to be a backbencher, I suddenly had time to spare for things that I had been denied for a number of years.

Still, I continued to urge my team of advisers to do everything necessary to clear my name. Rod McLeod continued to work on making the authorities come to grips with the fact that they'd targeted the wrong guy. And Glenn Hainey was trying to get the court to remove my name from the search warrant.

One of the truly amazing things about all this was how seamlessly the McGuinty government continued to do its work. Dwight Duncan, who was the energy minister and government House leader, gave up those portfolios and immediately assumed my old role as minister of finance. I had been working on a Fall Economic Statement when I resigned, and Dwight didn't miss a beat delivering the statement on the very day that we had prepared for. He also said something very classy to me after his appointment: "Greg, I'm just keeping the seat warm. You'll be back." It was particularly touching, since Dwight had always wanted to be Ontario's first ever finance minister who represented a Windsor riding.

One of the things I missed the most during this period of quarantine was my relationship with the boss. Dalton and I were certainly never pals. We were not drinking buddies. But what we had was as good and close a working relationship as any I could ever have imagined. I cherished that, and for the time being it was gone. At times I wondered whether he would ever want me back as his lieutenant or whether I would ever qualify again.

Then six months into the ordeal, an event took place that touched me to the core, an embrace the likes of which I had never experienced in politics. On April 4, 2006, some of my closest friends organized an event, "Dinner in the Piazza," which they styled as a *friend-raiser* — in contrast to the hundreds of political fundraisers that were so much a part of our political lives. They just wanted to show the world that I still had a few friends out there who believed in me, the RCMP investigation notwithstanding. Greg Wong was the event's chief organizer. The team rented the Paramount Banquet Hall in Vaughan and packed it with 1,100 people. It was a totally magical evening. Three premiers were there — Dalton McGuinty, David Peterson, and Bob Rae — and Bill Davis sent a note. At the evening's conclusion I even allowed myself to think that maybe the scar of this criminal investigation wouldn't be so permanent after all.

I also came to appreciate the Opposition leader of the day, John Tory. He was incredibly gracious. He made it clear to his caucus that there were to be no unsubstantiated attacks on me while on the "disabled list." I'll never forget that. I didn't have much of a relationship with the NDP leader, Howard Hampton, but one of his MPPs, Rosario Marchese, and I continued to have a lovely, chatty friendship. I soon came to realize that, actually, if I had to, I could have a very happy life without being a well-known provincial minister. That insight turned out to be very helpful two years later, when I would deal with the issue of resigning as finance minister again, albeit for wholly different reasons.

If Tuesday, October 11, 2005, was the worst day of my political life, then Thursday, May 18, 2006, may have been the best. It was the eve of the Victoria Day holiday weekend and I was home alone. The phone rang at about 10:30 in the morning. It was Lynn Mahoney, from Gowlings.

"Greg, I've got some good news," she said. "We've won!"

Oh, my.

We both started crying on the phone. It was just amazing how my emotions started to flow after suppressing them for all those months. After the call, I continued to cry inconsolably for half an hour. I couldn't stop. I called my friend and senior political assistant Sharon Laredo and cried with her on the phone all over again. She then marched over to McGuinty chief of staff Don Guy's office, shared the news with Don, and said, "It's time to put Greg back in Cabinet."

"I'll talk to the premier," Don replied.

Shortly thereafter, my phone rang again. It was Dalton.

"Greg, why don't you come to Queen's Park tonight and we'll get you sworn back in as minister of finance," he said.

Several things flooded into my head at that moment. I realized this calm in my personal life would now come to an end. I also thought, *If I'm sworn in tonight we'll destroy the long weekend plans of thirty or so bureaucrats in the ministry of finance, who will have to prepare to get me back up to snuff for Tuesday morning on a whole host of issues.* So I said to my premier, "Dalton, how about we just leave it till Tuesday?"

"Wow!" he responded. "In all the time we've worked together it's been *you* who always presses me to get things done sooner rather than later. This is the first time you've ever wanted to delay something!"

The day after the Victoria Day holiday, I got my old job back. At the first Cabinet meeting the following day, there was a touching round of applause as I entered the room, and then we were back to business. The first time I saw Dwight Duncan, he said: "Greg, it's good to have you back. I was just watching over it for you. I hope I left things in good shape."

My reply: "Dwight, you will be back here. Trust me."

Less than a year and a half later, Dwight Duncan, the member for Windsor-Tecumseh, was sworn back in as minister of finance, a job he ultimately held for six years — the longest-serving Liberal finance minister in a century.

A week after my return to Cabinet I had my first question period. NDP MPP Andrea Horwath asked our health minister, George Smitherman, a question about child-care tax credits. Since the question was more related to finances than health policy, George flipped the question to me. As I rose to answer, the members present in the House began a round of spontaneous applause. I was really moved.

"I really appreciate this," I said to my fellow MPPs. And then, lest they might think I stage-managed the moment with George, I added, "I did not plant that question!"

One of the ironic postscripts to this saga took place four years after my exoneration. The RCMP contacted me, of all people, to be the lead witness in the case against Vic De Zen. At this point I wasn't a great fan of the Mounties, but I had promised in my submissions that I'd co-operate with them on the Royal case should they need me. So I made good on that commitment.

I spent three days in Oshawa, April 27 to 30, 2010, as a Crown witness in the case against Vic De Zen and his Royal colleagues. I was determined to be as forthright as possible in both examination and cross-examination. At the end of the day, however, I don't think my testimony added much strength to the Crown's case. Indeed, I never thought the Crown had much of a case to pursue.

In December, after an eight-month trial, each side gave its summary arguments to Justice Richard Blouin. Immediately after those summations, Judge Blouin asked the defendants to rise. "I find you not guilty. The charges are dismissed. You're free to go," he said.

Incredible. Most judges in cases of this size reserve a decision and force the parties to wait weeks or months to hear the verdict and the judge's reasons. Justice Blouin tossed the whole thing out lickety-split. If there were ever a clearer indication that this case never should have gone to criminal court, I haven't seen it.

All told, the case may have cost taxpayers and the Royal Group $20 million or more — public money not well spent. I'm sure there's plenty of white-collar crime in Canada, but not in this case.

The case against Vic De Zen represented a serious but temporary setback for him. Eventually, he sold the business for $13.00 a share — a significant drop from the 2002 value of $32.00 per share. But Vic is a trooper. He signed a non-competition agreement for three years. As soon as the agreement expired, he started a new plastics business. A couple of years ago, Vic invited me up to see the new company. Remarkably, he had seven hundred thousand square feet of plant capacity in Woodbridge, with seven hundred employees. He wooed back many of the customers he once had with Royal. I don't think Vic will ever again run a public company. All those rules just aren't for him. But once again, he's become one of the leading manufacturers of plastic extrusions in North America with his new company, Vision Group — a true testament to his being one of the country's great entrepreneurs, particularly given the turmoil he went through.

I've been asked over the years whether I've really gotten over this whole Royal escapade. I've seen cases where bad things happen to people in politics and they never do get over them. They are left embittered for the rest of their lives. It's like an itch that does not go away.

I never wanted it to be like that. I am no longer haunted by the great misadventure in my political life. In fact, if you go to my Wikipedia page, the fact that I had to resign as finance minister because of an RCMP criminal investigation isn't even in the opening paragraph.

But it is in the second paragraph.

8

Politics and the HST

In no time at all, I was back up to speed in the minister's office on the seventh floor of the Frost Building. My staff seemed happy with my return and I was thrilled to be there. Indeed, that tired old adage — what doesn't kill you only makes you stronger — was true at least as far as the Royal adventure was concerned. I felt a renewed determination and devotion to the various missions that were my responsibility.

There was plenty of work to do. I had been lending a hand to former Ontario NDP premier Bob Rae in his campaign for the federal Liberal leadership; the legislature was in the midst of a busy spring agenda; work needed to begin on the Fall Economic Statement in which we would report a strengthening Ontario economy; the York subway file needed constant attention; and, of course, we needed to begin preparations for the October 2007 general election.

I was preoccupied by one thing. After the general election I would no longer be Ontario's minister of finance. I would be leaving a job that I truly loved. I had told no one, not even Dalton, about a commitment to Kate to step down after the election. The plan was to serve just one term and then return to some semblance of a normal life with our kids and growing number of grandkids. With each passing week I could hear the clock ticking just a smidge louder.

Preparations for the 2007 election campaign began in earnest in the fall of 2006. We were determined to replicate the structures and training that had worked so well for us in 2003: a leader's circle and a campaign committee with the usual subcommittees — platform, organization, communications, opposition watch, and others. This time around, however, candidate search would be less of a burden. We held the majority of seats in the legislature and most of our incumbents would be running again. And, of course, we were in government and firmly in control of the province's political agenda. Not surprisingly, the catchphrase for Campaign 2007 would be "Change That's Working" — and it worked for us.

The campaign went off without a hitch. It was Dalton's third campaign, and the extent to which he had grown as a leader was evident from the moment the writ was issued. We were able to overcome the mantra of "liars" and "promise breakers." Across the way, John Tory and the Progressive Conservatives got badly mired in his ill-advised promise to provide public funding for faith-based schools. In June most polls had us tied with the Tories at about 35 percent; but after the PCs' commitment on religious schools hit the streets, their numbers began to drop steadily.

For me, at least, the outcome had never been in doubt. When all the votes were in, we had secured a second majority mandate with 42 percent of the total votes cast. The Tories took just 32 percent. We lost just one seat. The PCs actually picked up two seats, despite losing 3 percent of their total vote compared to 2003. But John Tory himself lost his attempt to move from a rural riding to one in the middle of the city, when Kathleen Wynne defeated him in Don Valley West. The NDP was still very far behind with only ten seats.

Amidst all of the euphoria following our electoral success, I became ever more fretful about my future. I had fallen in love with my work, and our government was doing well. We had brought Ontario's finances back into balance. We were making the improvements to health care and education we had promised. I was blessed with a tremendous staff. We were, in my mind, World Series champions. But it was now time to confront the inevitable.

The new Cabinet was to be sworn in on October 30, and I had not been invited to the table where those decisions were being made. The premier simply assumed that I would be staying on in finance. On October 24, Kate and I had one final discussion where I suggested the possibility of staying on for six months to do just one more budget. She was rightly despondent. This was no time to break yet another promise. After as restless and tortured a night as I had ever experienced, I realized that it really was time to keep a promise. It was time to go.

In the morning I phoned my chief of staff Diane Flanagan to break the news. "Diane, I'm not staying," I told her. Her answer: "That's okay, neither am I." She was trying to make light of this bombshell. I then told my long-time adviser, Sharon Laredo, who pleaded with me to reconsider. She wanted to orchestrate a more graceful exit. "I'm worried about how people are going to interpret this," she told me. "It may look as if you're being disloyal to Dalton to quit Cabinet so soon after an election victory."

I called the premier and told him the news.

"How about six more months?" he asked.

"That's not going to happen," I replied.

"Should I speak to Kate?" Dalton asked me.

"Not a chance," I said. The premier couldn't have been more gracious. He understood completely.

I called in my staff for a meeting later that day. There were nearly two dozen people in the minister's boardroom. It became quite a teary affair. We had become a tight-knit group dedicated to a common cause. Angelo Spano, my personal assistant and a Queen's Park staffer since driving for David Peterson, was a case in point. We had become very close. We had been with each other every day and knew that was coming to an end: a teary affair indeed.

Our communications team, led by Sean Hamilton and Michael Arbour, put together an announcement for the next day, Friday, October 26. I know most politicians express the desire to "spend more time with my family" as the reason for leaving politics. In my case, I think the claim was credible and there didn't seem to be any skeptics in the Queen's Park Press Gallery. Many of them had known me for some time. When I reminded them that I was now over sixty and my wife's sister had just died of cancer, the notion of a loudly ticking clock counting down the healthy years we had left together didn't seem so far-fetched. Kate appeared with me at the news conference, and together we walked out into the rest of our lives. I suddenly felt at ease with the decision.

So it was that my successor and predecessor in finance would once again become my successor. Dwight Duncan was returning, as I had advised him he would in May 2006, as Ontario's minister of finance. Within a few months he would begin work on one of the most challenging assignments our government ever attempted — the creation of the Ontario Harmonized Sales Tax, or HST.

The introduction or reform of consumer taxes has typically confounded governments around the world, no less so in Canada and in Ontario. In 1961, the government of Premier Leslie Frost introduced Ontario's first ever retail sales tax (RST). The rate was 3 percent, and of course people disliked it so much they nicknamed it "the Frost Bite." Over the intervening years, the rate has gone up and down, depending on economic circumstances. It was at 8 percent when we came into government. Treasurers of every bent have relied on the RST because it's a dependable way to raise significant revenues to pay for government programs. When I was minister of finance, the RST raised $17.5 billion a year, almost one-fifth of our total revenue stream. Citizens pay tiny amounts of tax on every doughnut, newspaper, or pack of gum they buy. And, of course, they pay a great deal more on new cars. Add it all up, and it's hugely important to the province's bottom line. Over the years, the RST had been applied only to goods, but never services — and even then, when political expediency called for it, many governments exempted various goods from the tax to encourage their purchase (such as child car seats) or to give cultural industries a break (such as eliminating the tax on books).

The politics behind sales taxes are awful. I remembered all too well the efforts by David Peterson in 1990 to cut the sales tax by one point in the dying days of the campaign. People thought we were trying to bribe them with their own money, and Liberal fortunes plummeted.

Of course, the most famous national example of sales tax reform came just before that, when Prime Minister Brian Mulroney tried to replace a bad, clunky, hidden 13.5 percent manufacturing sales tax with a lower, visible, more efficient and fairer Goods and Services Tax (GST) on almost everything, including services. The opposition characterized the move as something akin to the end of civilization as we knew it, when in fact it was simply tax reform policy that was long overdue. Still, the federal Tories got clobbered for doing it. The GST went into effect three months after our 1990 election loss, and even though the next federal election was more than two years away, the Progressive Conservatives never recovered. It was one of the many reasons why the federal PCs fell to two seats in the 1993 national election. And, as everyone knows, once the Liberals under Jean Chrétien took over, they kept the GST in place despite promises to the contrary during the election.

That's the lesson all over the world. Governments that try to make meaningful sales tax reform always pay a price at election time, but the new government rarely goes back to the former system. In opposition they will demonize whoever is in power for daring to make unpopular changes to the tax code, but once in power they change nothing. The only exception I can think of was by Christy Clark in British Columbia, who, when she took over for Gordon Campbell as premier, repealed the HST. It was bad policy but good politics. It probably helped Clark keep the BC Liberals in power, but it has unquestionably weakened that province's economy.

That was the political context within which Duncan began his research. The economic context was even more dire. By mid-2008 Ontario, along with most of the industrial world, was falling into what ultimately became known as the Great Recession. The Ontario economy was contracting at an alarming rate; the entire auto industry was edging toward insolvency; capital markets were freezing up; and, of course, provincial revenues were falling drastically. The only remaining beacon of strength was industrial, commercial, residential, and infrastructure construction, assisted in part by the joint efforts of Ontario and Canada to fund stimulus projects across the province.

What Dwight needed urgently was an initiative that would strengthen the fundamentals in Ontario. He turned to sales tax reform. This was not surprising. Most economists in the province, certainly those in the ministry of finance, knew full well that the single most effective measure to improve economic performance in Ontario would be to scrap the existing retail sales tax and implement a single harmonized sales tax in partnership with the federal government. This had been on the agenda of finance ministry bureaucrats for years, and a great deal of modelling had been done beyond the prying eyes of their political masters. But the political climate had never been right. Indeed, when the matter was raised with me while I was in finance, I jokingly suggested that it would be less painful for me to simply put a bullet through my skull on the front steps of the legislature.

Now however, the negative forces of the Great Recession and the con-
sequent contraction of Ontario's economy created a kind of perfect political storm that might allow for courageous restructuring of the province's
consumer tax system. Dwight and his officials, in partnership with Jim
Flaherty and his federal department, began to flesh out the architecture
of a new Ontario Harmonized Sales Tax.

After the new Cabinet was sworn in, I quickly adjusted to my new role
as a backbencher and relished the new time and space I had to enjoy some
of life's other delicacies. Still, I was not completely idle. On behalf of the
government I led a province-wide study of tourism, something that we had
committed to in the 2007 campaign. We reported our findings and recommendations on February 11, 2009, in a report entitled *Discovering Ontario:
A Report on the Future of Tourism*. It was well received by the industry
and led to important restructuring of tourism management across the
province. I also headed an all-party select committee of the legislature
charged with reviewing the Election Act and the Election Finance Act.
Bill 281, which followed the committee's report, made some important
changes to Ontario's election law without delving into more controversial
reforms such as Internet voting or proportional representation.

I also agreed to stay on as campaign chair for the 2011 election. At
the time, it seemed a fair distance away. And I continued to play a role,
somewhat diminished, as an adviser within the premier's inner circle.
For that purpose, Peter Wilkinson, now the premier's chief of staff, and I
would meet every Thursday for lunch in Peter's office. The agenda would
include anything and everything that might affect the political fortunes
of the government and the party.

But, as was appropriate given Cabinet secrecy and the confidential-
ity of tax reform, Peter never shared the extent to which tax reform was
barreling down the track. I convinced myself and advised anyone who
inquired that, at best, Budget 2009 would announce a white paper commission on sales tax reform.

That was what I thought. What I discovered along with the rest of the
world on budget day, March 26, 2009, was that the McGuinty government
proposed to replace the retail sales tax with a fully harmonized HST and
to have it fully in place by July 2010. I felt a combination of shock, anger,
and betrayal.

I just couldn't see how we could get over this. The Ontario Health Premium was a bitter enough pill for people to swallow, particularly after we'd promised not to raise taxes. But the fact was many people didn't pay the premium at all, and the financially better off bore a higher burden, as they should. But this was different. A harmonized sales tax would put a higher financial burden on every Ontarian. The biggest change would be on services, historically exempt from provincial sales taxation. Now we proposed to add an extra 8 percent to the cost of haircuts, piano lessons, and legal services, to name just a few. And all this after we had promised *yet again* in the 2007 election campaign not to raise taxes! Politically, I was convinced we were dead, particularly since the new blended tax would go into effect in July 2010, just over a year before the next election campaign.

Rob Benzie of the *Toronto Star* visited me late on budget day to ask whether we, as a party, had gone completely nuts. I didn't have a good answer. I wondered aloud to my staff and others why we had decided so early in life to commit political suicide. For a brief moment I considered resigning both my seat in parliament and my role as campaign chair, but only for a brief moment. I remembered that for the past decade I had relentlessly preached the importance of solidarity among the team, particularly in the face of adverse political winds.

The first time I had an opportunity to meet Premier McGuinty and Don Guy, our campaign director, after the HST announcement, I said simply: "I understand why you've done this. But I have no idea how we're going to survive politically."

The premier's response was classic McGuinty. "Let's just keep going. We'll get through it."

I decided to swallow my personal misgivings, because any hint of resigning would have represented a body blow to both the team and the initiative. I imagined the impact of a damaging headline: "Sorbara Resigns over HST." Any hint of dissension might have encouraged other Liberal MPPs to follow suit. We just couldn't afford that.

Ever so slowly my perspective began to change. In part, I was impressed by the views of economists and commentators from across the political spectrum who argued that the HST was an important component — in the case of some analysts, an essential component — of a viable strategy for Ontario's economic recovery. In part, I was regularly browbeaten by former advisers like Arthur Lofsky, who insisted that, electoral politics notwithstanding, the HST would be good for Ontario.

Early on, the premier sent a "calculated" request through Peter Wilkinson for me to speak in support of the HST at the first caucus meeting following the budget. Obviously, they wanted to dispel any notion that the former finance minister was offside or that, as campaign chair, I was resigned to the notion that we were dead in the water. That speech, which by all accounts went well, served as the first step on my personal road to rehabilitation. I began to see ever more clearly the real wisdom of the reform. All of us in caucus and the party now needed to join forces to sell the HST across the province as best we could.

Two things helped us on our mission. The first was the appointment of John Wilkinson, Peter's brother and the MPP from Perth, as minister of revenue with a clear mandate to sell the benefits of the HST in every town, large or small. He was the perfect choice, the happy warrior who kept hitting away at the benefits of the new tax system in clear and convincing language. The second was the extent to which the Progressive Conservative opposition to the HST rang hollow. After all, the project was developed and implemented in partnership with a Conservative federal government led, for these purposes, by Jim Flaherty, a former Ontario finance minister who knew the file as well as anyone. Moreover, the former provincial PC leader, John Tory, regularly expressed his support for the tax on his much-listened-to daily Toronto radio program.

We also benefited from the expertise with which the new HST was put into place on July 1, 2010. It would be difficult to overplay what an enormous bureaucratic assignment such a new system represents. Every business in the province is affected; every cash register in every store needs to be reprogrammed. New rules need to be explained, an army of administrators need to be trained, and the entire system must work to near perfection on day one. The success of the implementation stands as a tremendous tribute to the army of civil servants who actually did the work. That success moderated to some extent the level of popular anger that was inevitable as consumers started to pay higher taxes on so many of the services that are part of daily life.

As preparations for Campaign 2011 began to take shape, we were not as badly shell shocked as we might have been. We noted wherever and whenever we could that, for all their vitriol, neither opposition party was proposing in its platform to repeal the HST. Instead the opposition parties used the HST to bolster their rhetoric that the Liberals were chronic liars who ought not to be trusted with a third mandate. The polling data suggested that their message was getting through.

But there was another reality that haunted me even more. Thus far in Canadian political history, no government that had implemented a GST or HST was re-elected in the subsequent election. My job was to see if there was a way in which we could buck that trend.

9

A Major Minority: The 2011 Election

Throughout my life some of my closest friends would routinely chide me for being an optimist on steroids. As we approached Campaign 2011, I needed as much optimism as I could muster. Realists from every corner were putting our prospects of winning a third mandate somewhere between slim and none. I had to admit they had a point. The impact of the recession on Ontario's economy, the implementation of the HST, anger about wind farms, and the general sense that Liberals had been around long enough all played against us as the election approached. Yet I was determined to remain hopeful — even optimistic.

I privately wondered whether we could once again rely on our opponents doing something ill-advised to help turn the tide. In 2003, the PCs put out a press release calling Dalton McGuinty "an evil, reptilian kitten-eater from another planet." The intention may have been benign humour, but all it did was demonstrate the mean-spiritedness of the Tories. In 2007, the PCs ran on a platform of extending public funding to faith-based schools, an extremely unpopular idea and another unforced error for the Tories. Could we rely on our opponents to make yet another major mistake?

Actually, I thought the prospects were likely. Both opposition leaders — Tim Hudak for the PCs and Andrea Horwath for the NDP — were rookies. It's always an advantage to have led a province-wide campaign, and in this case McGuinty was on his fourth, while the others had never done it before. I thought that was a real plus for us. I also thought Tim Hudak was making no discernible impression on the Ontario electorate, and I was even hearing from Conservatives that they had doubts about his ability to break through.

Still, the realists would hasten to point out that in the summer of 2011 we were, according to some polls, as much as fifteen points behind the Tories. On the crucial question of whether the province was on the right track or the wrong track, almost two-thirds of Ontarians said we were on the wrong track. Those numbers represented an awfully high mountain to climb. Perhaps surprisingly, there wasn't as much nervousness in the caucus as one might have expected under those circumstances. McGuinty led with his typical quiet determination and managed to ease the anxiety of caucus quite effectively. Throughout his tenure as premier, he had a master's talent for managing the emotional swings of the caucus and the party. His often-repeated mantra was "never too high, never too low," and it aptly described his overall approach to his work and his life.

As with previous elections, it was my responsibility to help find those bright new candidates to carry our banner. The challenge was all the more daunting because this time thirteen of our sitting members were set to retire. A year out, many potential candidates who might otherwise be eager thought our prospects for re-election were rather dim.

One of the best places to find prospective candidates is on the municipal councils of the province. Chances are if they have any political ambition, they'll be open to exploring the possibilities of running for a "more senior" level of government. It's good training and good for their profile. Moreover, they don't have to quit their local council jobs to make a provincial (or federal) run.

It was with that in mind that I began to pursue Moya Johnson. Moya was a salt of the earth municipal councillor for Halton Hills and the Canadian Urban Institute's Local Hero Award winner for 2009. I made three trips to visit her in an effort to convince her to run. "Moya, you have to do this," I pleaded. But Moya needed something from me. And here's where politics came into play. The Georgetown Hospital expansion was on the ministry of health's to-do list. But its approval was moving at a snail's pace. Moya insisted that we get that hospital expansion unstuck before she would consider putting her name on a ballot as a Liberal. So I contacted our health minister, Deb Matthews, and made the pitch to accelerate the Georgetown Hospital expansion. I asked her to put some fire under the project. Deb moved the hospital expansion up the list, and presto! we had a candidate for the riding of Wellington–Halton Hills who even before voting day had achieved something for her community.

We also wanted to win back Thornhill, just north of Toronto. It had flipped back and forth between Liberals and Tories since 1999. We had lost it to Peter Shurman in 2007. Again, we had a wonderful candidate in mind. Bernie Farber had an outstanding career with the Canadian Jewish Congress, fighting anti-Semitism and racism wherever they existed. Even though he supported public funding for religious schools (a policy belonging to the previous Tory campaign plan and very much *not* in our thinking), his own children went to public school. And unlike Shurman, he actually lived in the riding. Farber said he was open to being a candidate, but he needed a decision on provincial funding for a Jewish charitable organization called Zareinu. Zareinu was a gem of a community organization, providing services to special needs children, many very seriously disabled. I was straight up with Bernie. I told him the charity was a private one and therefore unlikely to be eligible for public funding. But I promised him we'd look at it. Getting someone of Bernie's calibre to run for us showed we still had plenty of game left.

In Welland, the legendary maverick Peter Kormos had decided to retire from provincial politics after twenty-three years. We thought a solid candidate might have a shot at taking that seat away from the NDP. So we approached Benoît Mercier, the head of ACFO, the Association canadienne-française de l'Ontario. Benoît came highly recommended. He was soft-spoken but had a very high profile in Welland. We also thought having an articulate francophone candidate would strengthen the entire team, particularly in ridings with large francophone populations such as Glengarry-Prescott-Russell and Timmins–James Bay. There was significant risk for Benoît. He was giving up a career as the head of a respected, non-partisan organization. But he said yes.

In Windsor, we needed a new candidate to replace our veteran cabinet minister Sandra Pupatello, who shocked many of us in the summer of 2011 by announcing she was retiring from politics. Sandra was forty-nine years old, clearly a future leadership hopeful, and her departure from Queen's Park led many to believe she didn't think we had another victory in us. Sandra routinely won her Windsor West seat by massive margins. It wasn't a Liberal seat. It was a "Sandra seat." Without the right candidate in her place, we feared we could lose it.

Our candidate search team settled on making a pitch to Teresa Piruzza. Teresa was from Windsor, had attended university in Windsor, had a long history with the Ontario Liberal Party, and worked for the city. "Call her," the team said to me. I made the case as strongly as I could. "Teresa, the work of an MPP is very much like the work you're already doing for the city. You've got a good following. Being from the Italian community helps. We really want you to run."

Teresa was interested, but she had two young children and was concerned about being too often absent from them. "The challenges with kids are the same no matter what you do," I told her. "You don't have to worry about being in Cabinet. You won't be in Cabinet. You won't want to be in Cabinet! As a backbencher you will find the workload to be moderate and you'll have time to get your bearings." Teresa said yes.

One day, a woman named Tracy MacCharles came by to see me at Queen's Park. Wayne Arthurs, our MPP in Pickering–Scarborough East, was retiring, and she wanted the nomination to run in his stead. Frankly, I was expecting to have yet another of the hundreds of conversations with prospective candidates who had no chance of getting onto a ballot for us. But Tracy was different. She had worked for the provincial government. She knew Queen's Park. She was vice-president of human resources for the corporate and information technology divisions of Manulife Financial. I could also see that Tracy wasn't healthy and learned she was suffering from breast cancer. This was her second encounter with the disease. Her first run-in was as a teenager — bone cancer in her left leg, which left her with an apparent limp.

She looked right at me. "Greg, I get around a bit more slowly than others do," she said. "But I have the energy and determination to do this." I believed her. After years of candidate recruitment, I always asked myself, "What kind of vibe do I get from this person? Do I sense that they'll have the energy for this kind of work?" With Tracy, I sensed the sky was the limit. She was wonderful. She wanted us, and we wanted her.

But we had a problem. The Pickering–Scarborough East Liberal riding association wanted another candidate to replace Wayne Arthurs. And Wayne's long-time friend and assistant Bill Hepburn (whose brother Bob is a columnist with the *Toronto Star*) also expressed interest in the nomination. Part of my job as campaign chair was to deliver bad news to people who didn't want to hear it, and actually convince them to accept another mission. I had to tell Bill that I was dashing his dreams of being the next MPP for the area. We had targets for female candidates that we were adamant about meeting. We also preferred Tracy MacCharles, plain and simple. Would Bill stand down in the party's greater interest and help us with other ridings in the Durham Region? Fortunately, he too said yes.

With each month I was more and more pleased at the quality of candidates we were attracting. It would be harder for our opponents to portray us as a sinking ship with this calibre of people lining up to run for us. And there's another point worth making here. In none of the examples above did any of the prospective candidates ask for anything for themselves. The public may be under the impression that when we recruit potential candidates we have to bribe them with promises of Cabinet positions and the like. It's just not so. Moya wanted a hospital expansion for her community. Bernie wanted help for a charity near and dear to his heart. The others didn't ask for anything.

I've only ever made one exception to the rule of not enticing a prospective candidate with a Cabinet job. Before our first election victory in 2003, I found myself at the home of former attorney general Ian Scott. Ian used to have a garden party every summer at his beautiful home at the foot of Castle Frank Crescent in Toronto. On this occasion, I saw Rob Prichard, who had finished a remarkably successful tenure as president of the University of Toronto and was now running the parent company of the *Toronto Star*.

"Rob, I don't generally do this," I told him, "but if you run for us, you'll be attorney general if you're willing. Or any other job in Cabinet, for that matter."

"Greg, I'm flattered," he replied, "but I'm on a mission right now and simply can't do it." A shame — Prichard would have been such a powerful candidate for us in 2003. But the reality was he already had a powerful job with a salary that exceeded the collective pay of the entire Cabinet.

In the three elections for which I was campaign chair, I was constantly on the lookout for talent. I never got tired of it. I loved trying to sell people on politics as a career path. And, of course, I also had an eye to the overall team we were trying to put together. Did we have enough female candidates? Was there a mix of cultures and languages? Could they do the job of a candidate or might they embarrass us? Much more often than not, we found candidates who made us very proud: Michael Coteau (Don Valley East), Soo Wong (Scarborough-Agincourt), Helen Burstyn (Beaches–East York), Indira Naidoo-Harris (Halton), Cortney Pasternak (Parkdale–High Park), and Christina Martins (Davenport).

However, sometimes it wasn't so straightforward.

One day, my office got a call from John Tory Jr., the son of the former PC Party leader. "We'd like to talk to you about having Sarah Thomson run for you in the election," John said. My thinking was I'd like to talk to John Jr. about having *him* run for us. That would have made a helluva statement! Nevertheless, some on our team found the notion of a Sarah Thomson candidacy intriguing. We were impressed at the impact she had made with her run for the 2010 Toronto mayoralty, even though she had dropped out before election day. I didn't know her, but she seemed to be able to carry herself well and capture a disproportionate amount of attention for someone who'd never won anything and was polling in the low single digits. After she quit the mayor's race, she endorsed George Smitherman, our former deputy premier, so Liberals had reason to look kindly upon her. The more we thought about it, the more we thought Thomson's candidacy could work. And we had what we thought was a perfect riding in mind for her.

Political contests in Trinity-Spadina always capture a lot of attention. Federally, the riding had been held by the NDP's Olivia Chow since 2006. But the Liberals' Tony Ianno had held it for thirteen years before that. Provincially, the NDP's Rosario Marchese had held the riding since its creation in 1999. He seemed an unbeatable fixture in this part of downtown Toronto. However, we noticed a couple of things. First, his passion for being an opposition MPP was waning. And second, there were a lot of newly built condominiums in the riding whose inhabitants were not necessarily New Democrats. So we decided a successful Sarah Thomson campaign might very well unseat Marchese. She had high name recognition, a natural ability to campaign, and lots of energy. Unfortunately, it didn't take long for things to fall off the rails. Sarah's problems were classic. She wanted to run her own campaign. A series of campaign managers we sent in quit in frustration. She spent like crazy. She freelanced on policy. She put out a pamphlet advocating for a subway *under Queen Street*. I called her in.

"Sarah, you just can't do that," I told her. "First, it's almost impossible to build a subway under Queen Street. Second, of all the ridings in Ontario, which one do you think already has the greatest concentration of public transit? Yes, Trinity-Spadina. Third, what happens when the premier comes to campaign in your riding and the media asks him about building a Queen Street subway? He'll say no. Sarah, this isn't a second run for mayor. This is party politics and you're on a team."

Despite all of the problems during the campaign, Sarah Thomson nearly pulled off a victory. I still have a soft spot for her. I think as a more mature candidate she could still be a successful MPP. But in the campaign of 2011 she simply couldn't transform herself from a solo star to a team player.

One of our biggest breaks actually happened five months before election day. Stephen Harper made history by winning a majority government — the first prime minister ever to win a majority after winning two minority governments. I always regarded Harper's government as pretty right wing, and given the penchant of Ontarians to elect different parties at the national and provincial level, I thought it unlikely that they'd want two hard-right governments at the same time. So Harper in Ottawa shifted the balance in Ontario slightly in our favour.

I was happy with our team of candidates. Now, I wanted one last opportunity to influence the party's policy platform. So, at the last Liberal provincial council meeting before the election was called, I put a big idea on the table. Since this was the first election in the twenty-first century's second decade, I wanted the election to be very future-looking and to be about what Ontarians should aspire to in the *decade* ahead, not just in the term of the next mandate. The tag line for such a campaign would be "Ontario's Next Decade." I envisioned a campaign about reimagining our finances, our energy system, and our health-care system ten years into the future. And there was another big idea. Re-elect us, I suggested, and we will begin the process of eliminating tuition at the undergraduate post-secondary level. It may take ten years. It may take twenty. But we're clearly in an era where having a college or university degree is as essential to getting a good job as graduating from high school was two generations ago. Other jurisdictions had already led on this.

Let us have this grand educational mission, I thought. We can take a small step in year one, but let us begin the transformation of post-secondary education in Ontario. The idea would connect us, I thought, to young people and higher education. These were admittedly big ideas that excited me. Unfortunately, no one else could feel the spark. No one!

We were still trying to recover from the Great Recession. Money was too tight and politics in general had moved away from grand visions and into small, bite-sized policy ideas.

A move toward free tuition would not be offered in the 2011 Liberal election platform. However, the campaign team liked enough of the idea to offer students of families earning less than $160,000 a year a 30 percent reduction in tuition. The grants would apply to about 86 percent of the ninety thousand full-time students in Ontario's post-secondary institutions. Not bad. But not quite the grand vision either.

As the fall 2011 election approached, I became more optimistic. The premier and the new finance minister did well at managing the effects of the Great Recession. They exuded a level of experience and confidence that I thought people would grudgingly accept. True, our numbers weren't as buoyant as in the past, but I worried little about polls. I saw them as a reflection of what people thought yesterday. I was more concerned about what they'd think tomorrow, and how we could influence that.

Still, there were a few things that concerned me. The Green Energy Act was causing us endless headaches in rural Ontario. Our government had made the decision to deny municipal governments the right to regulate the installation of giant wind farms in their localities. That violated one of the cardinal principles that had kept the Tories in power in Ontario for forty-two straight years — keep local political leaders in the tent with you.

Another issue related to gambling. Finance Minister Dwight Duncan had appointed Paul Godfrey, the one-time chair of Metro Toronto Council, as the chair of Ontario Lottery and Gaming. Godfrey, a well-known Tory, had a vision of redesigning the business model of the OLG, including building a new convention centre, hotel, and five-star casino on Toronto's waterfront. Duncan signed on to the plan without any real assessment of the political consequences. Another part of the Godfrey plan was to eliminate the OLG's subsidy of the horse racing industry. Sadly, we began to implement the policy well before the election. The reaction in rural Ontario was immediate. My first ever friend in politics, Dennis Mills, called me to say we were destroying eighty thousand jobs around the province — the kids who feed and wash horses and clean out barns. "We will do everything in our power to overturn this," said Dennis, who was now with a group called Racing Future Inc. "Don't you realize how this is going to bite you in the upcoming election?" he mused.

Premier McGuinty visited Lieutenant-Governor David Onley on September 7 and asked him to draw up the writs for an election to be held October 6, 2011. I liked where we were in terms of policy and candidates. I liked our leader a lot more than either of the other two. With each campaign, Dalton was becoming more confident in his own abilities. I prayed one of the Opposition leaders would make a mistake.

And then, Tim Hudak did.

In our election platform was one line offering employers tax breaks if they'd hire skilled new Canadian citizens who lacked Canadian job experience. The cost of the program amounted to less than 0.01 percent of the budget. But the Tories seized on that seemingly insignificant expense and accused us of favouring "foreign workers" ahead of native-born Canadians. The Conservatives thought they had a brilliant "wedge issue."

They attacked us mercilessly, hoping a sort of xenophobia would set in. But we counter-attacked hard and established an alternative narrative. We managed to portray Hudak and his minions as petty, unfeeling bigots. Yes, some of our Liberal candidates feared the Tory attacks would hurt them and they told me so. But by far, the PC approach was offensive to our base, and both the premier and I took aim. McGuinty blasted Hudak wherever and whenever he could. The campaign set up an event for me at Ryerson University in Toronto where I continued to fight back. I ripped into the Tories for misrepresenting our proposal and playing cheap politics with the plight of new Canadians. We completely turned the issue around. I told our candidates: "Don't apologize for our platform. Attack your opponent at every turn on this. Tell people this bigotry has no place in the province of Ontario."

On September 27, the party leaders held their televised debate. The debate format had never been McGuinty's strongest suit. I didn't think he had to win the debate — he just had to prevent too many pucks from getting into the net. Everything was marching along without much fuss until McGuinty suddenly turned on Hudak and hammered him out of the blue with the "foreign workers" story. Hudak was on his heels from then on. Eventually, I became as grateful to the Tories for this unforced error as anything I'd ever been grateful for in politics.

We caught another break as well. In an effort to show how stressed the health-care system was, Andrea Horwath told a story during the debate about how her eighteen-year-old son couldn't get a cast put on a fractured elbow that he'd injured in a skateboarding accident. Horwath claimed the hospital said a cast was too expensive and someone would show her son how he could wear a sling instead. Hamilton General Hospital staff were said to be outraged at the misrepresentation by the NDP leader, who eventually had to backtrack entirely on the story.

The most important decision the campaign team had to make was whether to try to bury our association with the Green Energy Act or wear it with pride, despite its flaws. The decision was driven by the man in charge. Dalton McGuinty insisted Ontario had to stop using coal, reduce our demand on oil, and embrace the future of green energy. He would hear of no equivocating or obfuscating of our commitments. He saw a future of more wind and solar generation, less natural gas generation, and no coal generation at all. Many people approached me, begging me to try to convince the premier to ease up on this issue. But he wouldn't hear of it, and I agreed with him, not because I was such a believer in green energy, but because our leader was always better at campaigning on issues in which he truly believed. So in a move that surprised many observers, we didn't hide our green energy commitments; we doubled down on them, frequently visiting wind and solar manufacturing plants, putting the focus on the jobs we would create in the green energy industry. It'll be a long time before we know whether our government's efforts to create a viable renewable energy sector will pay dividends for Ontario. However, politically, I have no second thoughts about the focus we put on that issue in 2011.

Meanwhile, Hudak's efforts to demonize us by taking advice from the so-called know-it-all kids in the PC backrooms backfired badly. Their campaign seemed to consist of calling the premier a liar. They looked and sounded mean-spirited. They offered little that was positive. Then they compounded their problems a few days before election day with a pamphlet drop in selected Toronto-area ridings decrying some Toronto District School Board anti-homophobia programs. First the Tories came out against foreign workers. Now their homophobia was on display. For the third consecutive election, the PCs would fail to win a single seat in the city of Toronto.

On election night I felt good about our prospects but uncertain as to how the numbers would roll out. I knew what we were trying to do was truly historic. No Ontario premier had won three consecutive majority governments since Leslie Frost in 1959. I watched the returns come in: we came oh-so-close. We lost seventeen seats and slightly less than 5 percent of the vote. But we still captured fifty-three seats — just one short of a majority government. *One seat short!* Under the circumstances I was happy with the result and considered it an important victory, while acknowledging that the minority parliament to come would make for some challenging times for our government. I'll also admit I was pleased to see the returns from Vaughan, where I managed to defeat my former protégé Tony Genco by more than ten thousand votes.

There were some ominous signs on that night, however. The PCs picked up twelve seats for a total of thirty-seven, while the NDP improved significantly, adding seven seats for a total of seventeen. Out of 4,000,000 votes cast, we still took 100,000 more than the Tories. But our vote collapsed in rural Ontario, and we lost some good people, including John Wilkinson, who had done such good work getting the HST passed. John lost his Perth-Wellington seat by just 630 votes out of more than 33,000 votes cast. The green energy focus no doubt helped solidify our numbers in urban Ontario, but they just as certainly doomed our candidates in the rural parts of the province.

I paid particular attention to the people whose candidacies I had championed. The record was mixed. Bernie Farber came close in Thornhill, but ultimately lost to Peter Shurman by 2,740 votes. Moya Johnson was crushed in Wellington–Halton Hills by more than 12,000 votes. In Welland, the NDP held the riding in spite of Peter Kormos's absence. And poor Benoît Mercier didn't just lose, he came third, capturing less than 20 percent of the vote. In Trinity-Spadina, Sarah Thomson lost to a twenty-one-year veteran of the legislature by just 1,075 votes. Had she been a slightly more disciplined candidate, we might have had our majority.

But I was thrilled with the outcomes in two other ridings. Tracy MacCharles swept away her Conservative challenger in Pickering–Scarborough East by almost 5,200 votes, taking 47 percent of the vote in the process. She is one of the most likeable members in the legislature, and in 2013 the new premier, Kathleen Wynne, made her minister of consumer services. Similarly, Teresa Peruzza won Windsor West with more than 41 percent of the vote. It wasn't a Sandra Pupatello–like landslide, but Teresa defeated her NDP opponent by almost 3,600 votes. She too would learn the ropes on the backbench for sixteen months and then find herself in Wynne's Cabinet as minister for children and youth services. I couldn't have been prouder to see these two women do so well.

Throughout the campaign I had numerous conversations with none other than the eighteenth premier of Ontario, Bill Davis. Mr. Davis hadn't been an elected politician in more than a quarter of a century, but he was still actively interested in provincial politics, and I was delighted to be one of his "informants," keeping him abreast of what was happening in the campaign from the Liberal perspective. He never let me forget he was a committed Tory, but he was also happy to offer advice to anyone who wanted it. The day after the election, I called Mr. Davis. Referring to our new status as a minority government, I said, "It looks like we're now in territory you were quite familiar with for four years."

"Greg," he interjected, "it was six years." Right he was: 1975 to 1981.

I had an idea. "How would you like to come to Queen's Park and meet with Dalton?" I asked him. Much to my delight, Mr. Davis agreed. I was freelancing here. I hadn't bounced the idea off of anyone in the premier's office, let alone the premier himself. But I thought Premier McGuinty would benefit from whatever wisdom Mr. Davis could impart. Frankly, I didn't mind the notion of having the media record pictures of my Liberal premier and a Progressive Conservative legend breaking bread together. From all accounts, the two premiers had an excellent meeting a week after the election. McGuinty was able to get some valuable advice on how to make a minority parliament work from the one living politician in Canadian history who arguably did it better than anyone else. And it was another reminder that, although Mr. Davis was a former PC Party leader, the true inheritor of his moderate, oftentimes progressive course was Dalton McGuinty, the Liberal, not Tim Hudak, the Progressive Conservative.

Finally, the Premier's key advisers needed to resolve one more issue: what to do about being one seat short of a majority. Some thought we should make entreaties to certain opposition members in hopes of luring someone to cross the floor. Others suggested putting the Speaker of the legislature, Dave Levac, in Cabinet, and urging an opposition MPP to run for Speaker. I was against both ideas. I didn't mind us being one seat short. "If we do either of these things, we'll just create other problems," I told them. "Every single MPP in our caucus will be able to hold the premier hostage on one issue or another. Any disgruntled MPP who felt the premier didn't talk to him enough or seriously consider him for Cabinet would have us over a barrel."

This was no academic concern. This very thing had happened in Manitoba in 1988. One of NDP premier Howard Pawley's backbenchers voted against the government's budget. The government fell, Pawley resigned and left politics, and the PCs under Gary Filmon won the ensuing election. The backbencher later admitted he voted against his own government's budget because the premier refused to put him in Cabinet, as per his request.

I was determined that this fate would not befall Dalton McGuinty. One seat short of a majority we would remain.

Two local campaigns in election 2011 warrant special attention, one in my own riding of Vaughan and the other in Eglinton-Lawrence. We were never at risk of losing either seat. What set them apart from the remaining 105 ridings was that in both cases the Progressive Conservative candidates were high-profile Liberals who had jumped ship to play for the other side. Both had been Liberal activists since they were teenagers, with notable records of achievement. In my view, both made very bad decisions, effectively torpedoing their own political prospects and ending friendships that had lasted for decades.

Tony Genco was seen by Liberals everywhere as a true party stalwart. He had a keen eye for politics and a real sense of the issues. Right out of school he joined the team of federal Liberal cabinet minister Robert Kaplan and worked his way up through the ranks. He hung out at Queen's Park through the 1980s, and when I won my first election in 1985 I hired him to work in both my constituency office and downtown at the Ontario legislature. I always thought Tony had excellent political instincts, and we became very close over the years.

In 1995, when I stepped away from politics for the first time, Tony asked me whether he should try to seek the Liberal nomination and replace me as the MPP for York Centre.

"My advice to you, Tony, is to wait," I told him at the time, "because Al Palladini will probably win this seat for the Conservatives." Tony took the advice and went to Ottawa to work on Parliament Hill. In 1999 he did challenge Palladini as the Liberal candidate, ran a solid campaign, and narrowed the margin of the PC victory by a thousand votes.

When Dalton McGuinty asked me to seek the Ontario Liberal presidency after his 1999 election defeat, it was Tony who was adamant that I had to accept the invitation. He convinced other talented young Liberals such as Sharon Laredo and Steven Del Duca to join the effort, and together they created an organization that surpassed my 1992 leadership campaign organization.

After Palladini died it was Tony who insisted that I become the Liberal candidate in the by-election. "You're president of the party. You have to do this."

He was very persuasive. Tony chaired the by-election campaign that sent me back to Queen's Park as president of the party, chair of the upcoming election campaign, and MPP for Vaughan-King-Aurora. Through it all, Tony was a constant source of great advice and political instinct, so much so that I invited him to join the party's executive council. He became a terrific insider and called me day and night to share his insights, which I welcomed.

Tony's solid relationship with Liberals both provincial and federal eventually paid off with an appointment as president and CEO of Downsview Park in Toronto — but after the Conservatives took power in Ottawa in 2006, Tony got the axe.

Then, in September 2010, Liberal MP Maurizio Bevilacqua stepped down from his federal Vaughan-King-Aurora seat, causing a by-election. I encouraged Tony to seek the nomination, which he did. I wrote him a cheque. I even chaired his campaign. It was his second run for elective office, and he faced a very tough challenge: Conservative star candidate Julian Fantino, the former chief of the Toronto Police Service.

Bevilacqua routinely won his seat by thousands and thousands of votes. In fact, I think he still holds the Canadian election record for margin of victory. But clearly the tide was turning. The Conservatives were now winning "905" ridings, on the outskirts of the city of Toronto. In November 2010, Fantino edged Tony by just 964 votes.

Under normal circumstances, such a close showing might entitle the candidate to a second kick at running for the seat. Certainly, Tony felt he had earned the right to challenge Fantino again in the general election, which happened just half a year later.

But in politics, people talk. And the talk around Tony's by-election campaign was that despite the closeness of the contest, the federal party wasn't happy with him. There were rumours that he didn't work hard enough and mistreated volunteers. My advice to him at the time was "Don't push it." If the party wants a different candidate, let them have one. The Liberals weren't going to win the seat anyway, not against an incumbent Julian Fantino and rising Conservative fortunes. I told Tony all of this.

But something changed. Tony had what might be called a classic "Italian" reaction. He felt his honour had been impugned and he was offended at the way the federal party was treating him. Shortly thereafter, I got a call from him in which he said he was mulling his options, one of which was to jump to the Conservatives. I was in shock.

"Tony, that would be a really, really, really, crazy thing to do," I told him. "That's a very dangerous trick in politics that almost never works. You've been a Liberal since you were a teenager. Everything about you is affiliated with the Liberals. You shouldn't do this." Tony thanked me for the advice and said he'd get back to me with his decision. As we ended the conversation, I couldn't help but feel he was now a lost soul, who was at the beginning of a downward spiral that would not end well.

Tony didn't call me back. Then I heard he was working for Julian Fantino.

But the story gets crazier. Next thing I knew, Tony decided to become a provincial Progressive Conservative candidate *against me* in the October 2011 Ontario election! I was absolutely dumbfounded. And heartbroken.

I had nurtured Tony Genco in politics as he did me. I counselled him. I took advice from him. And I didn't want to run against him, only because I knew I would beat him and beat him badly. I didn't want him to suffer through that experience.

From a purely political point of view, Tony's running against me was actually good news. I could now afford to spend more time in the rest of the province, doing my job as election co-chair. All-candidates' debates in Vaughan were difficult for both of us. As Tony tried to defend Tim Hudak's right-wing Tory platform, I merely had to say, "Well, a year ago when I chaired your campaign as a *Liberal*, you had a different set of principles. How could those principles change so dramatically in just a year?" There simply was no answer to that question.

Furthermore, there were probably two hundred or more dedicated Liberals in the riding that had been signed up *as Liberals* and organized by Tony over the years. They were utterly appalled at what he'd done. That base of support would have nothing to do with him. Again, not to play stereotypes, but Italian Canadians have no patience for political turncoats.

I can only assume that Tony decided to run for the Tories in the 2011 provincial election because he thought I wouldn't run. He thought Tim Hudak would win the election and that he'd therefore have an easier time winning what would have been an open seat. He miscalculated on both fronts. As a result, I pledged to myself that I would not allow *that guy* to take *my seat* on behalf of *another party.*

And I didn't.

Even though I lost 9 percent of the vote compared to 2007, our campaign still managed to capture 53 percent of the total vote, good for a margin of victory of more than ten thousand votes. It was a very big win.

After I left politics for good, Tony ran again for the Progressive Conservatives in the ensuing by-election in September 2012. He ran against Steven Del Duca, another of the young kids who were part of our team for so many years. I knew Steven would win. It was closer, but once again Tony lost. Steven held the riding for the Liberals by nearly 5,800 votes. He is now the minister of transportation in the Wynne government and one of the rising stars in the Ontario Liberal Party.

I don't see Tony Genco anymore. We don't speak. I inquire after him when I see mutual acquaintances. I think the Tories used and abused him. And I take no joy in saying I was right — the Tony Genco story in politics did not end well.

I wasn't as close a friend to Rocco Rossi, but I knew him pretty well. He had an outstanding resumé, a strong academic background, and a commendable record as a leader, particularly as CEO of the Heart and Stroke Foundation of Ontario from 2004 to 2009. His career always seemed to be going up and up and up. Like Tony, he'd been a Liberal since his teenage years. I can remember Senator Keith Davey saying on numerous occasions, "We've got so many bright, young kids in this party like Rocco Rossi. In fact, Rocco could become PM some day."

One of Rocco's best friends in politics was Michael Ignatieff, who in February 2009 asked Rocco to become the Liberal Party of Canada's national director. Essentially, the job was to get the party ready for the next federal election. Because it was a minority parliament, no one knew when that election would happen. But there had been elections in 2004, 2006, and 2008, so getting up to speed as quickly as possible was imperative, since the next election was almost certainly just around the corner.

One day in the spring of 2009, Rocco wanted to get together with me at the now defunct Bistro 990 at Bay and Wellesley Streets near Queen's Park. Given that I was the Ontario Liberal campaign chair, I thought he was going to hit me up for my Rolodex, or at the very least, for some advice.

Instead, Rocco asked me to leave my provincial seat and run for the federal Liberals in the next election. "Michael Ignatieff is going to win the next election," he told me, "and you'd make a great federal finance minister." I said, "Rocco, I'd rather rot in hell than be in federal politics, that far away from home." Then I turned the tables on him. Assuming he intended to run in that next federal election, I asked, "What seat are you considering running in?"

"Actually," he said, "I'm thinking about running for mayor of Toronto."

I was stunned. I didn't say this to him, but I certainly thought to myself, *How could he say that?* Rocco had a job that permitted no compromise in one's political loyalty or self-interest. In my view, you need to be the chief barker for your party, not use the job of national director to burnish your credentials for a mayoralty run, which would be only a year and a half away.

"Rocco, you can't win the mayor's race," I told him. "You're smart. You're competent. And among a certain slice of the public, you're well regarded. But no one else has any idea who you are." I put it very starkly: "You will not win."

That was the moment when I started to have pretty significant doubts about Rocco Rossi. He just seemed to have a blatant conflict of interest as to which mission he was really committed to. Nevertheless, we got together a few more times after he became a candidate for mayor. I was happy to give him whatever advice I could, but I couldn't be an "official, masthead supporter" on his campaign literature. The fact was that one of Rocco's competitors for the mayor's chair was George Smitherman, my former Cabinet colleague and a former deputy premier in the Liberal government of Ontario. I simply couldn't support anyone else over George, given our history together in the McGuinty government.

The campaign unfolded much as I suspected. Rocco simply couldn't get any traction. His ideas weren't bad, but it became a two-person race between Smitherman and Rob Ford. Midway through the campaign, Rocco tried a Hail-Mary desperation play to capture some attention, given that nothing else was working. He ran some campaign ads that indulged in stereotypes about Italians and organized crime — stereotypes we've been trying to get away from for decades. The commercials certainly got Rocco some attention, but not the kind he wanted. The spots were panned, lampooned, and viciously criticized, and I wasn't surprised when a few weeks before election day he dropped out.

I heard through the grapevine that Rocco was upset with many provincial Liberals because so few supported his mayoralty campaign. But with George Smitherman in that race, he ought not have expected significant support from our camp.

After the dust settled on the municipal campaign, I met with Rocco again, but this time to talk to him about the pending Ontario general election in October 2011. I told him he'd made a name for himself through his mayoralty campaign, and his name recognition was now much higher.

I talked to this lifelong Liberal about several potential seats, including Trinity-Spadina and Davenport in downtown Toronto, where he'd be welcomed as a candidate. I even held out hope that York West MPP Mario Sergio might retire (he was seventy years old) opening up that seat as well. All three ridings had a significant Italian-Canadian population, and I thought Rocco could win any of them. I also added another seat to the list.

"Rocco, there's every possibility I won't run again, in which case maybe even my seat could be in the mix," I told him. I didn't promise him my seat. But I dangled it as a possible option depending on my own plans.

Next thing I knew, Rocco Rossi announced he was running for Tim Hudak's Progressive Conservatives. Again, I was both heartbroken and dumbfounded at the political folly of it all. And worse, he had chosen to run against my friend Mike Colle in Eglinton-Lawrence. The federal Conservatives had taken Eglinton-Lawrence away from Liberal MP Joe Volpe in the federal election earlier in that year. The thinking was if the provincial vote were to follow the same trend, the riding could fall to Hudak.

For my part, I found the choice inexplicable. Our internal polling showed the Liberals would have to lose fifty seats before Eglinton-Lawrence fell to the Tories, and we weren't going to lose fifty seats.

Not only that, but Rocco's decision created an incredible amount of blowback against him and the entire Progressive Conservative campaign. The day he announced he was switching teams, I got a dozen calls from Liberals who were appalled at Rocco's defection. Dennis Mills called to say he would do whatever it would take to help Mike Colle defeat the disloyal Rocco Rossi.

That reaction was typical. Liberals came out of the woodwork for Mike Colle, to ensure Rocco wouldn't win.

On election night, we Liberals did lose seventeen seats. Eglinton-Lawrence wasn't one of them. Mike Colle crushed Rocco Rossi by almost eight thousand votes.

Why did Rocco turn his back on more than three decades of Liberal politics to run for the Conservatives? My assessment is he figured the McGuinty government was out of gas and that Hudak was going to win. If Hudak did win, Rocco would be ideally placed to become finance minister in that government. I think Rocco also sadly had a very overblown assessment of his attractiveness and abilities as a candidate. I guess he figured no one could beat Mike Colle except him. He figured wrong.

I suspect the lesson of Tony Genco and Rocco Rossi is that ambition can be a very harmful toxin. In both cases, I think their decisions were fuelled by an excess of ambition and a miscalculation of what they perceived as a good political opportunity. But it wasn't an opportunity. It was opportunism. There's a difference. In the end, it was a shortsighted, misguided venture that has left both of them with very few friends in politics.

Since the election, I have had no relationship with either Tony Genco or Rocco Rossi. And that's really the saddest part of all.

Wrapping up the 2007 Ontario Budget Presentation.

With former Ontario premier Bob Rae at a community event
in Vaughan, 2004.

The 2010 Ontario Liberal Party Annual General Meeting, Toronto.

Premier Dalton McGuinty and I, pre-election rally in Vaughan, Ontario, 2011.

Election night in Vaughan, 2011.

Leaving Queen's Park following my resignation as MPP for Vaughan, August 1, 2012.

Installation as the thirteenth chancellor of York University, June 13, 2014.

Our annual Thanksgiving dinner at the family farm, Prince Edward County, 2012.

10

Departures

I met Dalton McGuinty shortly after he was elected as the only new member of the Liberal Caucus in the 1990 general election. The consensus view is he made no discernible contribution to the Parliament or the party during that first term. All the more surprising, therefore, that he was the long shot winner at the party's leadership convention in December 1996. I was one of a handful of former MPPs who voted for him through five ballots. Still, our lives did not really begin to intersect until after the election defeat in 1999 when he prevailed upon me to become the party's president. From that point on, we worked ever more closely together on a common cause, winning the next election and thereafter running a government dedicated to improving public services.

Given that relationship, it is not entirely coincidental that we each departed the political stage within months of one another. There, however, the similarities end.

My departure was without drama or surprise, a slow dénouement that began when I left finance in October 2007. His came about with a surprising and courageous announcement in October 2012 of his intention to step down as premier after nine years at the helm. It was made amidst the most vicious and slanderous attacks against the government and him personally that I had ever seen in more than twenty-five years at Queen's

Park. His decision had a selfless quality to it that captures succinctly the quality of his character.

First, then, the final scenes leading up to my own exit in August 2012. After the passage of the HST budget, I started to devote most of my political energy to what would be needed to win a third term in October 2011. Certainly the odds were not in our favour.

In the spring of 2010, the highest-ranking members of Dalton's inner circle held a deep background meeting at the historic George Brown House on Beverley Street in downtown Toronto. It was close enough to get to, but far enough away from Queen's Park to avoid prying eyes. The mission was to discuss a policy and political agenda that would carry us through the next eighteen months to the general election. Ontario was beginning to emerge from the Great Recession, but revenues were still significantly below what we were counting on. At that meeting, I was determined to advocate for a plan to come to grips with the province's finances. I wanted us to put something in motion that would eventually manage down expenditures and expectations. I even had a name for it.

My idea was to create the Ontario Commission on Public and Broader Public Service Compensation. The reality is, when you count it all up, probably 80 percent of what the province spends is on salaries. Think about it. If you take the fifty-or-so-thousand people who work directly for the province, and add the million-or-so people who work in the broader public sector (municipalities, universities, schools, hospitals, and the rest), that's just a huge chunk of what the provincial treasury funds. And 90 percent of those employees are unionized. So the idea was to create a blue ribbon panel that could do some deep analysis on reorganizing and restructuring what some people call "Ontario, Inc." I reminded everyone that simply freezing current wages wouldn't get the job done, because once the freeze came off, unions would do their level best to recapture what they had lost during the freeze.

The high-powered group of advisers that the premier had assembled included Shelly Jamieson, secretary to the Cabinet; Dwight Duncan, the finance minister; his chief of staff, Tim Shorthill; and Dave Gene, Chris Morley, Don Guy, Gerald Butts, and Laura Miller, all high-ranking members of the premier's political team. This group met only occasionally, but clearly, from my standpoint, it was an important get-together. We were now heading into the early days of pre-election planning. We needed the upcoming year to be marked by a positive economy and an aggressive plan to deal with the government's growing deficit. Our re-election chances in October 2011 would depend on our success in those two arenas.

As it turned out, the premier and finance minister didn't go for my narrowly focused commission on public service workers. They wanted something much broader. It took almost another year for the plan to crystallize in the form of a major budget announcement in March 2011. The government would tap economist Don Drummond, the highly respected twenty-three-year veteran of the federal ministry of finance and former chief economist of the TD Bank, to head the Commission on the Reform of Ontario's Public Services. The mandate was vast. Drummond and his team were to look to the very core of how government worked, what services it ought to be in, and what services might be better delivered by the private sector. Underlying it all was, of course, the strong need to cut expenditures. Don was Dwight Duncan's choice. I thought it was an excellent one.

With the 2011 budget now out of the way, the focus was clearly on our government's re-election efforts. Once again, I had to face an excruciating personal dilemma. I had made a tentative decision that the 2007 election would be my last. I even stalled holding my Vaughan riding nominating meeting until every other riding had a candidate. When asked, I simply said that as campaign chair I wanted to make sure we had our whole team in place before seeing to my own situation.

One day in late July, the premier's executive assistant, Tracey Sobers, called me. "I have Dalton on the phone for you," she said. The premier and I exchanged ten seconds of pleasantries and then he got to the point. "You are running again, right?" he asked me. Actually, it was more of a statement than a question. "Dalton," I replied, "you know I'm not." It wasn't the answer he wanted to hear. "I think you need to run again," he countered. "You can leave after six months, but you need to run again." I paused before responding, "Okay, I'll give it some thought."

I didn't need to give it much thought. I was a pretty high-profile player in the campaign. Dalton was my premier and I was his general in the field. I just thought there's no way to make a surprise exit. If after all my cajoling of others to run, all my efforts to raise money for the cause, all my cheerleading on behalf of Liberals everywhere, I decided to retire, I knew it would deflate the party. I could see how the opposition and media would have a field day. "Hey, Dalton," they'd say, "your own campaign chair doesn't think you're gonna win, why do you?" I just wasn't willing to run the risk of having that happen.

Up to the moment of Dalton's call, I had fooled myself into believing that I could bring our campaign team right to the goal line and then step aside and let someone else take us into the end zone. But I couldn't, and there was no way of getting around that. I called the premier back and confirmed I would be a candidate in my York Region riding for the seventh time.

The campaign itself had its moments. Unmasking the Tories on the issue of "foreign workers," debating my old friend Tony Genco in Vaughan, and making guest appearances in dozens of other ridings all inspired me. But my heart was not fully in it. Kate was seeing to matters on the farm. Having had hip replacement surgery the year before gave me considerably less bounce going door to door, and early on the reception from major donors was rather cool. Still, the overall provincial result was a third Liberal mandate, albeit a minority one.

The biggest difference with this new parliament was, of course, that we were going to need the co-operation of one of the other parties to get anything done. So before long, and thanks to my strong friendship with him, I developed a kind of back channel relationship with New Democrat MPP Rosario Marchese. After the Christmas break we'd meet periodically at a coffee shop at Dupont and Christie Streets near his Trinity-Spadina riding, to have informal "negotiations" in advance of the 2012 budget. I would bring ideas to him, he'd take them back to the NDP caucus, and we'd get a better sense of what budget items would fly and which wouldn't. The major issue in that budget was the demand from the NDP that a surtax be applied to those with a taxable income over $500,000. On the one hand I wanted to get from Rosario how deeply committed his party was to the surtax, and on the other hand I began to urge our side to accept the proposal despite the fact that, once again, we could be breaking a promise not to raise taxes. In our caucus, I asked the question, as one of the few at Queen's Park who would have to pay the tax, if I was in favour of it why should they not be in favour? Of course, I had another mission at these meetings. I wanted to find out what it would take to get Marchese to quit politics, since we were only one seat shy of a majority government. We didn't imagine bringing him over to our side. Rosario was a lifelong and committed New Democrat who had no appetite for jumping the ship he was on. We just needed the opposition to have one less voting member. So we regularly talked about the possibility of an appointment. The problem was that Rosie's aspirations were bigger than what was in my bag of toys. He mused about the chairmanship of the Liquor Control Board of Ontario, or the Ontario Lottery and Gaming Corporation, or Ontario Power Generation — very high-profile stuff. I thought, given his social democratic background, he'd be a better fit at the Workplace Safety and Insurance Appeals Tribunal, or the Social Assistance Review Board. He argued that those appointments would require too much work and too little profile. Rosie was a good spirit, and I suspect he never thought he'd be in the running for the LCBO, OLG, or OPG, but why not ask? Still, our relationship was very warm, and I think served a small but useful purpose in helping us get our 2012 budget passed, even if the NDP abstained rather than voting for it.

The last part of the spring session in the legislature was dominated by debate on the budget bill. As I got up on June 20, 2012, to speak in support of the budget motion, I knew it would be my last speech as an MPP in that chamber. I didn't have an official departure date in mind yet, but I knew the House would be rising and not returning until September. By then I'd be gone. So I spoke to Carol Price, a staffer in the chief government whip's office, and asked to be the final speaker on the bill. I was not more than ten seconds into my remarks when the interjections got so loud that the Speaker had to stop me to quiet the place down.

"Folks," he said, exasperated, "I know it's the last day of school, but could we keep it down, please? At least give the member the ability to say something." I was grateful for that. No use having your last hurrah drowned in a sea of catcalls.

"Thank you, Mr. Speaker. As I said, this is a rare opportunity for me. Generally, I leave legislative time to my colleagues in our party who are more articulate and have greater insight, but I relish the opportunity to be the final speaker on this very important budget bill."

Right up to the last minute, it looked as if our government would be defeated on the budget. We thought we had an agreement with Andrea Horwath, hammered out in her private meeting with the premier, only to learn after the fact that her meeting with her caucus left her now wanting more concessions. Our side was completely ticked off with her, and everyone doubted a solution could be found. But there was a solution, I said as I continued my speech.

I had high praise for Dwight Duncan, for the chairman of the finance committee, Bob Delaney, and for the minister's parliamentary assistant, Yasir Naqvi. I included the good work the opposition finance critics Peter Shurman and Michael Prue had done. I then turned to the quiet informal diplomacy that Rosario Marchese and I had undertaken. "We had no authority, but it was in his interest and my interest that we work out an arrangement. As a result of those negotiations — and I say to my friend from Trinity-Spadina, I think we played a small part. We helped in that process."

Then, a peek at the clock and I knew I'd have to wrap it up. "I want to take this opportunity, in the final words that will be spoken before we vote, to congratulate the 106 members of this legislature, who, notwithstanding the partisanship, saw a higher calling; notwithstanding the urge to win and to be seen to win, saw the opportunity to do the right thing and make sure that this government has a budget and this government has a financial plan and that there will be no election this fall."

My last words in the Ontario legislature were directed to the man who replaced me as the minister of finance and to Dalton.

"Finally, I want to congratulate, in a very personal way, the work that my friend and my successor the minister of finance has done over the course of the past nine months. I know the burden of that job. I know how much it takes to make sure you get it right, and I say to my colleague the minister of finance that we in this legislature and Ontarians across the province thank you, sir, and our premier for your dedication." And with that, I sat down to modest applause. Question period was about to begin.

The budget passed in a vote later that afternoon.

After my speech, I spotted TVO's Queen's Park journalist Steve Paikin up in the gallery, where he and other members of the media were observing the proceedings. I went up to shoot the breeze with him. Out of the blue, Steve asked me, "Was that your last speech in the legislature?" I smiled but didn't react. He then changed from a question to a statement. "I think that was your last speech in the legislature." I just kept smiling and changed the subject. It was, but I didn't want to take any attention away from the successful passage of the budget, even speaking with someone I'd known since my first foray into politics in 1985.

It was actually in early April that my chief political adviser, Sharon Laredo, started putting the wheels in motion for my official departure. She enlisted Diane Flanagan, Sean Hamilton, and, later, Danielle Paroyan to plan an appropriate send-off. On April 20, we gave Steven Del Duca the heads-up that I'd be leaving and that he should get his ducks in line to contest the subsequent Liberal nomination and by-election in Vaughan. But we were still looking for the optimal moment to make the announcement. We didn't have to wait long.

On April 27, our government surprised Queen's Park observers by appointing Elizabeth Witmer to head the Workplace Safety and Insurance Board. Witmer was the longest-serving female MPP ever, having first been elected in 1990. She was a red Tory and a fish out of water in Tim Hudak's small-*c* conservative caucus. She also gave me the perfect pretext for my own exit from politics.

Jean Chrétien was always smart like a fox when it came to holding by-elections. When he had one he thought he might lose, he tried to orchestrate another in a safer seat and hold both by-elections on the same day to prevent the opposition from gloating too much. I thought, *Let's do the same thing here.* I knew we had little chance of winning Witmer's seat of Kitchener-Waterloo (and we didn't), and I knew we'd hold on to my seat in Vaughan (and we did). In fact, if you add up the total votes in both ridings in those September 6 by-elections, we killed the Tories, which was the perfect storyline as far as I was concerned. The NDP surprised everyone by taking Kitchener-Waterloo, but they barely got their deposit back in Vaughan. In other words, we stayed with the status quo, which worked for me.

I told the Premier's staff of my intention to resign my seat, and to my delight, Dalton decided he wanted to make an appearance at my farewell press conference on August 1. We used the government caucus room on the second floor of the legislative building, where the premier had held many important news conferences in the past. In my remarks, I wanted to assure Liberals across Ontario that I was only stepping down as an MPP, and that I was staying on as election readiness chair to focus exclusively on a campaign that, given our minority government status, could come at any time. I'll admit that was a bit of spin.

With Kate beside me and many of my kids and grandkids in the room, I announced that it was time to go. I realized in an instant and with an uncharacteristic calm that, despite leaving work that I had loved, despite twenty-seven years on the battlefield, despite whirling memories of battles won and lost, despite missions left undone, and despite the inevitable loss of the camaraderie that only politics can engender, it was the right time to go.

The media have a wonderful way of reminding you that what might be important in your life isn't necessarily so in theirs. After my speech and the premier's, the first question from a reporter was to the premier about teacher contracts. Obviously, I was already yesterday's news!

The event went off without a hitch. Kate and I walked out holding hands, ready to march into the rest of our lives, and I felt good about it. Yes, I felt a tinge of sadness leaving the building. Even when I hated my work, which at times I did, I never forgot I was working in the most beautiful building in the province. I wanted to take in the sights, the touch, even the smell of the place one last time. I thought, *I'm really leaving for good. Next time I come here I'll need a security pass to get in.*

There was a comforting finality to it all. As we left the building, Kate said to me, "Well, I think that went all right."

It was just two and a half months later that Dalton announced his intention to step down as premier of Ontario. A remarkable twenty-two-year political career was about to end. But it ended amid a poisoned political environment that cruelly and viciously damaged the reputation of one of Ontario's most dedicated and competent premiers.

To go back to the beginning, it was, perhaps, a given that someday Dalton James Patrick McGuinty Jr. would put his name on a ballot and enter politics. But nobody expected that day would come as soon as it did.

The riding of Ottawa South had been a reliably safe Progressive Conservative seat since its creation in 1926, sending Tories to Queen's Park for more than six straight decades. But in 1987 the province put its arms around David Peterson and the Ontario Liberals and, for the first time ever, Ottawa South went red. The new MPP was Dalton James Patrick McGuinty Sr., a long-time trustee on the Ottawa Board of Education and English professor at the University of Ottawa.

I knew Dalton Sr. pretty well. He was one of my parliamentary assistants when I was a cabinet minister in the Peterson government. He was also incredibly outspoken in caucus. He had a marvellously extroverted sense of humour and a brilliant command of the English language. But Père McGuinty's foray into provincial politics was short-lived. On March 16, 1990, he suffered a fatal heart attack while shovelling snow in his driveway. He was just sixty-three.

As the story goes, the McGuinty family gathered to decide which of the ten McGuinty children would pick up the torch and try to hold the seat for the Grits. The oldest son said in jest, "It may as well be me. After all, we've got a garage full of signs with my name on them." And so the decision was made that Dalton Jr. would be the candidate in the ensuing by-election. But that by-election never happened. Premier Peterson called an early general election for September 6, 1990. While Liberals were going down in defeat all over Ontario, Dalton Jr. became our only new member, capturing a very respectable 46 percent of the vote.

During his early years in opposition, Dalton Jr. made little impression on events at Queen's Park. I recall his maiden speech in Parliament being singularly uninspiring. I certainly never thought of him as our future leader. In fact, there was considerable talk around Queen's Park about how little we were getting out of the new member for Ottawa South. Certainly, he was not particularly engaged in the big question of the day for Liberals — who would replace David Peterson as leader— nor in the discussions about how to rebuild the party in the face of such a devastating loss in 1990.

To no one's surprise, when it came time to pick a new leader in 1992, the McGuinty family support was split; his wife, Terri McGuinty, gave her support to Murray Elston, while Dalton cast his lot with Lyn McLeod. Lyn won the convention, I dropped out of politics, and the Liberals lost the ensuing general election to Mike Harris. But Dalton McGuinty held his Ottawa South seat in 1995, and with a much bigger margin than in 1990.

When McLeod stepped down as leader, the Liberals were into yet another leadership race.

Gerard Kennedy was considered the front-runner. He was the golden boy of the convention. I didn't know him except by reputation; he had little parliamentary experience. But a man I respected mightily, our former treasurer Robert Nixon, was in Kennedy's camp. There was probably an expectation that I'd support Joe Cordiano because we were both Italian-Canadians and Joe had supported me at the previous convention in 1992.

I didn't know Dwight Duncan at all, since he'd won his first election after I'd left Queen's Park. And then there was this McGuinty fellow. His speech wasn't bad. It wasn't fabulous. But he had a stature about him. Tall and slim, he presented well. We'd had almost no contact during the campaign. Certainly, he might have called me to ask for my support, but all these years later the call has left no impression on my memory banks. Was he ready to be premier? Probably not, but *none* of the candidates were ready to be premier in my view. For me the real question was which candidate had growth potential. That's what I was looking for, and I decided after the speeches that the candidate was Dalton McGuinty. So I made a bit of a splash when I marched into his box at Maple Leaf Gardens. I doubt I brought many delegates with me, but the decision was made.

As the contest moved deep into the night, my decision at first seemed pretty foolhardy. McGuinty came fourth on the first ballot and a *worse* fourth on the second ballot. But he hung in there, and somehow, in perhaps the strangest leadership convention of all time, he ended up on the final ballot opposite Gerard Kennedy.

I voted on that fifth and final ballot and then went home rather than stick around to hear the outcome. It was already the middle of the night, I was out of politics, and I figured I could catch the result on the radio. I still recall my sense of shock on hearing, at 4:30 a.m. on CFRB Radio, that McGuinty had won the day — or, more accurately, the night. My reaction: *Oh, my goodness, I actually picked the long-shot winner!* And with that I went to bed.

I had no role in Dalton McGuinty's first election as leader in 1999. I watched the debate on television, as so many others did, and felt strongly that McGuinty did pretty well. He withstood an unfair and blistering attack from journalist Robert Fisher, who hammered the leader in the set-up to his question with every cheap shot under the sun. Some thought it was the knock-out punch of the debate, but not me.

Then my phone started to ring. "He was a disaster," said one. "We've lost the election," said another. Despite the onslaught, I didn't really doubt my evaluation of things. McGuinty came on strong in the dying days of the campaign. In the new legislature (which would have twenty-seven fewer seats as a result of the Fewer Politicians Act passed by the Tories in 1996) the Liberals actually picked up an additional five seats — going from thirty to thirty-five — and 9 percent more of the total vote to end up at 40 percent. On the other hand, the Tories went from eighty-two pre-election seats to fifty-nine after the votes were counted. The NDP went from seventeen to nine. The writing, faint and distant as it was, was on the wall. Harris won a second consecutive majority government, but McGuinty was only 200,000 votes behind out of 4.3 million votes cast. I was happy for him. It was encouraging. In effect, it was really a trial run for 2003, when a significantly improved McGuinty defeated Ernie Eves to become Ontario's twenty-fourth premier. In 1996, I saw a politician who was not ready for prime time, but who I thought had the potential to grow. I saw some of the basics of good leadership — integrity, decency, humility, and intelligence. In the years that followed, I saw a leader who was determined to school himself on what needed to be done to set a new and better course for the province. He studied assiduously what was needed to improve health care, to strengthen education, to make Ontario an environmental leader, and to unite a dispirited party on a determined political mission.

By the time we won the 2003 election, Dalton and I were deeply committed to each other and the work we wanted to do. It wasn't a deeply personal relationship. We never socialized together. There were no baseball games or double dates. No golf games or tennis matches. I felt very comfortable with that. Given the demands of politics, we both seemed to prefer keeping our professional and personal lives separate. The more I looked around, the more I discovered what seemed to be the model for almost all of the premier's professional relationships. I think we both realized that it's possible to get completely consumed by ego and ambition in politics if you make it your entire life. Neither of us wanted that.

In some respects, McGuinty and I were each other's yin and yang. I am burdened with an excessively emotive personality. The premier is far more stoic. However, over the years, I saw that change somewhat. I did watch him become a warmer, less inhibited person.

I'm a baseball guy. He's a hockey guy. We'd have Cabinet meetings and the premier would start them by saying, "Okay, let's get through all of Sorbara's baseball analogies and then we can get down to business." I never could sell him on the magic of baseball. Mind you, he could never get me to embrace his "beloved Senators."

From the moment I became our party's president in 1999 until the premier finally announced his retirement in 2012, our relationship remained strong and confident. Through the eight years that we oversaw the work of a majority government he became more skilled at understanding and managing the public affairs of the province. Within his party he had amassed a huge amount of political capital. As a result, most members of caucus were willing to go to the wall for him.

From the outset he had a studious approach to the premiership. During discussions on the major issues of the day, whether health care, education, or nurturing a green energy industry, he was always the best-informed person in the room.

Equally important, he had an uncommon ability to inspire discussion and debate around the table and to reshape his own opinion based on what he heard. The sheer burden of work in the job description of any premier is very high. Early on in his tenure he learned to work hard and effectively. But he did the job at a tempo that made it appear that he was never tired.

Still, the demands of the job take their toll. The reality in today's Canada is that the energy of a provincial premier is typically spent within eight to ten years, even for the most driven and successful leaders.

Dalton's case was no different. All of us in the inner circle knew that the election of 2011 would certainly be his last. Were we to win he would step down eighteen to twenty-four months into the mandate. We were all the more determined to win that campaign for the party and for him. We did not want his departure from politics to come by way of an election defeat, as had happened to David Peterson, Bob Rae, and Ernie Eves.

Unfortunately, we were only partially successful. The October 2011 election results left us with a minority government, a new and more challenging experience for us and one that changed the timetable for the premier's departure. In this new environment, the government began to take a beating that outweighed anything in our previous experience. The focus remained the gas plant cancellations and the September 2012 contempt motion relating to our former minister of energy, Chris Bentley. Suddenly the possibility that the government would fall became very real indeed.

For Dalton McGuinty this created a unique dilemma. If, after the 2012 Thanksgiving weekend, the government were to be defeated in parliament, a general election would be called forthwith. That would mean that he would have to lead his party for a fifth time into battle. It was something that he was simply not prepared to do.

The solution became obvious. Rather than waiting for a bright moment twenty-four months into the life of this parliament when he could retire with orchestrated fanfare, he announced on the Monday following the Thanksgiving weekend that he would be stepping down as soon as his successor could be chosen. In the interim he would prorogue parliament to avoid another general election only one year after the last.

For me, this was classic McGuinty. If I am not prepared to contest another general election, he thought, then I have a responsibility to call for a "time out" to allow for a new leader to be chosen. Rather than worry about his own legacy he determined that the collective interests of his province and his party outweighed the criticism that would dog him for his abrupt departure.

And so, on Monday, October 15, 2012, I got a call from Dalton's long-time assistant Tracey Sobers asking if I would be available later that afternoon to take a call from the premier. I said I would. As I hung up the phone, I said to myself, "He's about to resign."

Later that afternoon, the call came in. "Greg, I wanted to give you a heads-up that I'm retiring," the premier said. And I was really touched that he made that call. After all, I was no longer an MPP and he was certainly under no obligation to tell me. Shortly after 5:00 p.m. that day, Dalton called an emergency caucus meeting to announce two things: he was quitting politics, and he was proroguing the legislature at the same time. He said he wanted a cooling-off period, as the temperature at Queen's Park had simply become too hot. This would allow the Liberals to have an orderly leadership convention, without the Tories' contempt motion constantly threatening to bring down the government.

Dalton McGuinty made the ultimate sacrifice for the Liberal Party's future success. He took the brunt of the fallout for the gas plant cancellation costs, for holding a hard line on teachers' negotiations, and for the contempt motion against the energy minister, and he tried to take it all with him into retirement. He wanted to give his successor an opportunity to change the channel. He sacrificed part of his legacy in hopes of giving his party a chance to fight another day. For that, and so many other things, he deserves our respect.

And, of course, the real McGuinty legacy is rooted in what he accomplished during his premiership. He oversaw the transformation of Ontario's education system, rated in 2010 as one of the world's best; a much more responsive and reliable health-care system; the refocusing of Ontario's energy system toward clean, renewable energy generation; environmental policies that included the creation of a GTA greenbelt; historic investments in infrastructure, including public transit in the GTA; and, year after year, increasing help for Ontario's vulnerable populations.

The intensity of relationships one forms in politics rarely survives once you're out of that cauldron. That's natural. But I expect the relationship I had with Ontario's twenty-fourth premier will endure for the rest of our lives. I thoroughly enjoyed working with him.

11

The Truth About Gas Plants

I was horrified at the way in which events unfolded following the premier's
Thanksgiving announcement. With each passing month the attacks on the
government and the newly retired premier intensified, driven by the issues
that surrounded the cancellation of two natural gas plants, one in Oakville
and one in Mississauga. It was entirely unprecedented and unjustified, a
sort of feeding frenzy stoked by opposition parties determined to crucify
the former premier and the current minority government, aided by two
Auditor General reports that preferred to play to populism, and promoted
by the provincial media who preferred to enhance the emerging myths
rather than to report the facts. In the 150-year history of Ontario there is
no precedent for the kind of vitriol and anger directed at a retiring first
minister — and it is all the more offensive because of the extent to which
the political mythologies about the gas plant cancellations so thoroughly
trumped the truth.

In a column written in February 1988, the great baseball author and
historian George Will makes the point that "most myths are impervious
to evidence." That is certainly the case in politics. Virtually everyone in
Ontario is familiar with the mythology surrounding the cancellations
in Oakville and Mississauga: that in the midst of the 2011 election campaign Dalton McGuinty summarily cancelled both contracts at a cost
of $1 billion and that he did so in order to save a handful of seats in

the area. The real story and the evidence are a markedly different tale.

The Liberals came into office in 2003 with a pledge to rid the province of the noxious pollution that spewed out of coal-fired electrical generating stations that dotted the province. Dalton McGuinty had initially promised as opposition leader to close all the coal plants by 2007. After the election we discovered we couldn't do that until we had an adequate alternative supply of cleaner energy ready to go and had refurbished some of our nuclear generators.

Most of our efforts to create that alternate supply went very well. Despite plenty of opposition and criticism, we also passed the Green Energy Act, which provided a subsidy to those willing to build solar- and wind-powered infrastructure for cleaner energy. Would people have to pay more for that power than they would have for electricity created by coal plants? Of course they would. But we were guided by two principles: first, a determination to be North American leaders in a cleaner mix of sources; and second, the significant savings in health-care costs, as fewer kids got asthma and fewer adults developed respiratory problems, thanks to less pollution in the air.

As part of our plans to end the province's reliance on coal, the Ontario government began to implement a plan to build twenty-one gas-fired electrical generating stations. One such plant was destined for Oakville, where, in September 2009, the Ontario Power Authority (OPA) awarded a contract to TransCanada Energy (TCE) Ltd. for a facility that would serve the urgent energy needs in a rapidly expanding part of the province. Under the legislation governing approval of new plants, it was up to the proponent to identify a potential site and up to the OPA to approve or reject the application based on a competitive bid process. The underlying purpose of the legislation was to take the politics out of the decision-making process so as to ensure that no political favouritism would prevail in the selection of the proponent, or the site, for that matter. In government parlance, this is known as a "best practices" approach. The Cabinet would have no direct responsibility to sign off on the contract approved by the OPA. In the view of the OPA, the site proposed by TCE in Oakville met all the technical, zoning, and environmental requirements for the plant. But the decision did not meet the political realities of the day for the people and the town council in Oakville. Within weeks of the OPA decision, opposition from the community became intense. The people of Oakville made an increasingly persuasive case that the plant was far too close to residential areas and schools. They made it clear that, should the decision not be reversed by Cabinet, they would pursue cancellation in court and would argue all the way to the Supreme Court of Canada if necessary. The residents recruited U.S. activist Erin Brockovich to support their cause. Soon there were suggestions that residents were prepared to sit down in front of bulldozers, should it come to that.

In the spring of 2010, an elite group of Oakville residents came to my constituency office in Vaughan to reinforce their outrage. These community and business leaders included the president of Microsoft Canada. They made it clear: the plant had to be cancelled, or else.

Ultimately, the government realized that it made no sense to engage in a protracted legal battle that could be very costly and take years to resolve, and that it could lose in the end, given the emerging new standards for urban planning. Our local Oakville MPP, Kevin Flynn, was firmly on the side of his constituents. Most important of all, long delays in reaching a resolution could put the energy needs of the western GTA at serious risk.

Given all these circumstances, in October 2010 — a full year before the 2011 election — Cabinet decided to cancel the Oakville plant. There was no concern that we were at risk in the Oakville riding, where Kevin Flynn had been a well-respected representative since 2003.

When the Oakville cancellation was announced, construction on the plant hadn't even started. There was no way to quickly determine what the overall cost of the contract's cancellation would be, since we didn't have an agreement on a new site, an estimate on what a new plant would cost to build, an estimate of what the courts might award TCE for breach of contract, or an estimate on how much more it would cost to transmit electricity from a new, more remote location. Eventually, the new Auditor General was asked to analyze the costs of the Oakville cancellation. Remarkably, she used some of the same negative assumptions as had been used by her predecessor in his April 2013 report on the Mississauga cancellation as well as some of her own. That approach led her to a $650-million potential cost for the Oakville cancellation. Rarely did the media report that those potential costs would be spread over a twenty-year period. The fact is, we won't know the *real* cost of the cancellation until the new facility is completed in Napanee, the estimate of moving power from that location to the GTA is determined, what other generating capacity might be developed over the next decade, and what trends might emerge in the overall energy market down the road.

One thing is for sure, however. We avoided building a gas-fired generating station on a site many felt was unsuitable in the first place.

The other controversy was in Mississauga, where the contract to build actually predated the Oakville contract. In 2005 the ministry of energy initiated negotiations with the proponent, Greenfield, which the OPA concluded some months later. At first, the site for the plant was supported by the mayor of Mississauga, Hazel McCallion, and her council. Unlike Oakville, however, construction was well underway on the Mississauga plant when the political pressure to cancel the project began to heat up. Seeing a shift in the political winds, Mayor McCallion did an about-face and soon led opposition to the facility. By this time, the province was in full pre-election mode and Mississauga community groups decided to make the gas plant an important campaign issue. The Progressive Conservatives and the New Democrats gave the plant's opponents their full support, arguing that the site was far too close to new residential developments, a school, and a hospital. Once the official campaign began, each of the two parties promised that, if it won the election, it would shut down the plant. Indeed, Tim Hudak held a press conference at the Mississauga site to announce that under a PC government the plant would be "done, done, done." There is no report as to whether the press asked him what the potential cost of cancellation would be.

The handwriting was now on the wall. The community groups had identified real issues as to the suitability of the site, the mayor and her council opposed it, and both opposition parties had committed to close the site should they be elected.

In that environment, on September 24, some two weeks before election day, the Liberal Party gave in to the political pressure from all sides and announced that the construction of the plant would be stopped and that the plant would be relocated to a more suitable site. Eventually, a replacement site in Sarnia was approved with the full support of that community.

Was the decision to cancel Mississauga driven purely by electoral considerations? Perhaps not. As campaign chair, I never believed that the re-election of our candidates in the area — Harinder Takhar, Charles Sousa, Bob Delaney, Dipika Damerla, and Laurel Broten — was ever at risk. Perhaps what really happened was that the process of a democratic election flushed out an issue for the citizens of Mississauga that needed resolution — in this case, in their favour.

After the election, Auditor General Jim McCarter was asked to review the cost of cancellation for the Mississauga plant. His report, premised on a series of negative assumptions, estimated the potential cost to be $250 million over a twenty-year period. My criticisms of the Oakville report (which was presented six months after McCarter's) apply equally to his Mississauga valuation.

In the aftermath of the election, in a new minority parliament, the opposition parties became determined to exploit the gas plant myths despite having supported the decisions in each case. Before long, the rhetoric became both outrageous and slanderous. The attacks in parliament — and the public frenzy that grew with each passing month — developed on four fronts: a contempt motion in the legislature directed at Energy Minister Chris Bentley, outrage that the government had lowballed the estimated costs of the cancellations, the alleged deletion of email by political staffers, and a criminal investigation launched by the Ontario Provincial Police.

The Bentley contempt motion alleged that he, as minister, had withheld documents from a legislative committee looking into the cancellations. But the only documents ever withheld were ones that might compromise negotiations between the OPA and the contractor whose project was cancelled. The attacks on Chris were vicious and relentless, and so dispiriting that he finally resigned his seat in parliament on February 8, 2013. The more immediate impact of the motion, introduced by the Tories on September 26, 2012, was to paralyze parliament. The debate on the motion was to have precedence over all other business in the House. The opposition parties had the minority parliament in a stranglehold. Their aim was to bring the government down and force a new election less than one year after the 2011 campaign. At the time it appeared that they might just succeed.

It was this paralysis that caused Dalton McGuinty to advance the date of his departure, and so on October 15, 2012, he announced that parliament would be prorogued and that he would be stepping down as premier as soon as the Ontario Liberal Party could choose a new leader. In essence, he took the fall with some faint hope that, under a new premier, the parliament, the government, and the party could survive.

By February 2013 the province had a new premier, Kathleen Wynne, but the appetite to embellish the gas plant myths continued apace over the next year and more. Months of committee hearings were held, during which the opposition used every available tactic to suggest corruption. The new focus was to somehow link the story to the new Wynne administration. In his testimony before the legislative committee, McGuinty made clear that it was his decision to nix the Mississauga plant and that he would make the same decision today, given the negative impact the original sites would have had on the surrounding communities.

For all her good intentions, Premier Wynne did little to dispel the growing myths. Her first months in office were marked by far too much defence and far too little offence. Rather than defending decisions that represented the higher standards for municipal planning in dense urban areas, she decided to apologize and to do so repeatedly. The quality of her apologies simply strengthened the misconception that the plants were cancelled for purely partisan reasons at a cost of $1 billon.

It was a mistake, in my view, for the McGuinty government to make public the early estimates generated by the OPA of the actual costs to be incurred by the cancellations. There were far too many variables, too many unknowns, and too many long-term assumptions to put a realistic number on the table. The original lowball estimates of the OPA caused the government to fall into a trap and to suffer renewed political embarrassment with each succeeding upward revision of costs.

It was predictable that the Tories and the NDP would portray themselves as crusaders against corruption. That is an essential element in this sort of drama. But this, too, is a myth. When the Oakville plant was cancelled in 2010 there was no word of complaint from either party. Why would there have been? They were advocating for its abandonment.

A year later, during the 2011 election, both the Tories and the NDP were aggressively campaigning against continuation of construction at the Mississauga plant. Each party promised to shut it down if elected — not on condition that the cost of cancellation would be within certain parameters, but unconditionally. Of course, neither party did any analysis of the cost of cancellation before making its promises.

The story developed an even more intriguing plot when it was discovered that hundreds or thousands of emails were deleted by staffers in Premier McGuinty's office as they prepared to leave government with the premier. Now allegations of "cover-up" were added to those of corruption. This gave the myth a truly Watergate flavour.

Alas, the truth is far less titillating. The truth is that the contents of every one of those emails remains securely stored on the government's central computer system, available at any time to those who need to review their contents. This was confirmed by Informational and Privacy Commissioner Ann Cavoukian, notwithstanding that in an earlier report she had condemned the government for deleting all emails relating to the cancellations. In essence, she initially played into the myths and later offered no apologies when she reported that no records had actually been lost.

Finally, the myth-makers point to the entry of the OPP into the "gas plant scandal." Regrettably, there was little reporting of what it was that the OPP was actually investigating. The police force's issue was a small and simple one. Did David Livingston, then the chief of staff of the premier, commit a breach of public trust when he allowed a contracted technician access to government computers to delete the computer copies of emails? Did he somehow put the government at risk by permitting such unauthorized access to government information? The narrow scope of the OPP's work was confirmed to Dalton McGuinty when he was interviewed by the OPP after his departure from parliament.

The truth about the gas plants is that the McGuinty administration cancelled Oakville in 2010 and Mississauga in 2011 because in each case the siting of the plant was inconsistent with emerging standards for industrial installations within urban areas.

The other truth is that the uproar that developed after the 2011 election helped bring about Dalton McGuinty's departure from office somewhat earlier than he had originally anticipated.

Regrettably, the gas plant myths — impervious to evidence — left a temporary stain on the tenure of an Ontario premier who dedicated himself to his province for almost ten years with integrity and achievement that will serve as a standard for decades to come.

Still, with the damage done, it was now time for a changing of the guard.

12

Premier Kathleen Wynne

With Dalton McGuinty's departure from Ontario politics, I knew that my time with the Ontario Liberal Party wouldn't last much longer. Every new leader wants his or her own team. Clearly I was Dalton's guy and I knew that whoever succeeded him would want someone else to take on the political responsibilities I'd had. I was fine with that. I agreed to stay on in those roles on an interim basis, until a new leader could select the right people to replace me and the team I worked with.

The leadership convention was set for January 25, 2013, at what was now called the Mattamy Athletic Centre at Ryerson University, but which for eight decades everybody called Maple Leaf Gardens.

By this time I had become somewhat of an éminence grise within the party. One by one, those who were considering a run for the leadership came to seek my advice.

The first was Yasir Naqvi, our member from Ottawa Centre. Born in Pakistan, Naqvi immigrated to Canada at age fifteen. He was only in his mid-thirties and had taken over the presidency of the party in 2009. He'd been an MPP since 2007 and was widely seen as a rising star in the party. Naqvi wondered whether I thought his time had arrived. He assured me that he wanted to run not to be the "ethnic candidate" but rather to win. His ambition probably touched something inside me, given that twenty years earlier I was also trying to convince Liberals that I was in the race to win, and not merely to be the "ethnic" or "Italian" candidate.

When Yasir asked me whether I thought he should run, I told him the same things I would eventually tell all the candidates who sought my advice. First, there's nothing in politics like running for the leadership of your party. It's the World Series of politics. It's exhilarating and exciting. Second, don't run if your entire self-worth is wrapped up in it. You try to win but you've got to be prepared to lose. Only one candidate will win, and if losing is going to destroy your self-image or your pride, or break your heart, don't do it. Third, running is an excellent way to get to know the grand diversity of the province. You'll visit every corner of its immense expanse. You'll get to know the grassroots of the party. Above all, you need to figure out why you want the job and what you'll do with it if you get it.

I left the meeting convinced he was going to run. As it turned out, he decided against it. He and his wife had just had a new baby and the timing wasn't right. He was also very young and could afford to wait till next time.

I also got a call from former cabinet minister David Caplan. David's mother Elinor had been in David Peterson's Cabinet with me back in 1985. She had also been a federal cabinet minister in one of Jean Chrétien's governments. David had great political instincts but had fallen on his sword, resigning his position as health minister when eHealth expenditures became the subject of public controversy. David was now out of politics and wanted to set up a meeting to get my advice on running for the leadership. The meeting never happened. David must have sounded out others, realized the mountain was too high to climb, and begged off.

I considered that part of my job here was to encourage as many solid candidates as possible to run. I wanted to show the province that leading the Ontario Liberal Party was still a desirable job. I didn't want Ontarians to think the leadership of our party was a poisoned chalice, with all the controversies the new leader would have to manage. A vigorous leadership race would also bring many new members into the party.

The first person to see me who eventually *did* run in the 2013 Liberal leadership contest was Eric Hoskins. I'd always been fond of Eric, ever since he had contested and won the 2009 by-election in St. Paul's to replace Michael Bryant. I gave it to Eric straight: you're articulate, you're passionate, but in this race you will be considered the dark horse. You haven't been in the party very long, but if you have the energy to fight the fight, then do it.

Next, I met with Gerard Kennedy. I had to admit I couldn't really understand Kennedy's candidacy. He had left Queen's Park in 2006 to seek the federal Liberal leadership but that adventure did not exactly end in glory. In that contest Kennedy showed underwhelming support on the first ballot and then moved 90 percent of his delegates to Stéphane Dion, helping Dion become leader. Some pundits believe that move was designed to deny the federal leadership to Bob Rae and leave open to Kennedy a second shot should Dion not succeed. It hurt many of us who believed that Bob was the best choice for federal Liberals. Kennedy lost his federal seat in the 2011 federal election but declined to seek a seat in the provincial campaign later that year. Now, to everyone's surprise, he wanted to lead the party again. I did not tell Gerard I thought it was impossible for him to win, although that's what I was thinking. Still, he'd improve the quality of the debate on the issues during the contest, so I was happy to have him join the race. But I also knew his years away from Queen's Park would hurt his candidacy, and told him so.

"I think I can handle all of that, and I think I can win," Kennedy told me. He had a very positive attitude, a lot of devotees, and, at the very least, I thought he'd bring some people back to the party.

Sandra Pupatello and I had a conversation about her candidacy, and it mirrored the one I had with Gerard. Sandra had decided to step away from politics prior to the 2011 election, presumably thinking that some distance from the McGuinty government would serve her well if the party were looking for a significantly different leader. But some delegates would regard that move as quitting when the going got tough, and not having a seat in the legislature would be an added complication for her candidacy.

Harinder Takhar, at that time our minister of government services and chair of management board of Cabinet, also sought my advice. I made it clear that I would be happy to see him get into the race. Harinder would bring a lot of new members to the fold. He had strong credibility in the South Asian community. I also had a bit of a soft spot for Harinder. Again, he reminded me somewhat of my own experiences in 1992. I felt a need to prove to the Italian-Canadian community that one of their own deserved

178 · GREG SORBARA

to be playing on the biggest stage provincial politics had to offer. I'm sure Harinder felt the same way.

Charles Sousa and I had a chat. I thought he had the requisite ambition to seek the leadership. He brought significant support from the Portuguese community and from Peel Region. Some people, though, were concerned that Sousa's candidacy would bring unwanted attention to the gas plant we had cancelled in Mississauga. At his campaign kickoff, Sousa was asked by reporters scrumming him after his announcement why anyone would vote for him. After all, cancelling the gas plant was done in part to save his seat. Wouldn't his candidacy be a constant reminder of a failed policy? On the contrary, he said. He had lobbied against the plant in caucus, he had lobbied against it in Cabinet, and he was delighted to be able to deliver for his constituents. The issue never became an albatross for the Sousa campaign.

I wasn't the least bit surprised when Glen Murray called to discuss his potential candidacy. I'd always had a somewhat strained relationship with Glen. I feared he was too ambitious for our good and his own. It worried me during the lead-up to the 2010 Toronto mayoralty campaign that Glen was actively measuring support to become the city's new mayor. He'd only joined our provincial Liberal team in February 2010, replacing George Smitherman in a Toronto Centre by-election. Six months later he was in Cabinet. The rumours of his interest in the mayor's job that eventually went to Rob Ford suggested to me that he was putting personal ambitions ahead of an unbending commitment to our party. Glen's candidacy for leader was interesting insofar as he was by far the best at putting new ideas on the table and bringing passion to the candidates' debates. Unfortunately, his campaign never developed enough real traction, and in time he dropped out in favour of fellow Toronto MPP Kathleen Wynne. His decision certainly surprised me because I thought for sure that he wanted to experience the romance of giving "the speech" on convention day.

One candidate I truly wanted to see *in* the race was Deb Matthews. I've always had enormous regard for Deb's abilities. She had a clear understanding of provincial issues and she could have brought true passion to the race. When Deb told me she was actively considering a leadership run, I told her, "You'd be a great candidate and I'd be thrilled if you ran."

Ultimately, she decided against it, opting instead to become Kathleen Wynne's campaign co-chair.

As for Kathleen, well before McGuinty stepped down as premier, she had told me that when the time came she intended to be a candidate for the leadership of the party. Soon after the race began she called to confirm she was in.

Of all the people I talked to about the leadership, there was only one that I actually discouraged from running: my successor as finance minister, Dwight Duncan. A lot of people were urging Duncan to run for the prize. He'd been a successful finance minister and an MPP for almost two decades, and he had a lifetime of work in the party beyond that. He was a great performer in the legislature. Dwight ran in the 1996 convention, losing to Dalton McGuinty, and had that experience to draw upon. Were he to enter the contest, he almost certainly would have been the front-runner.

There were a number of factors that I wanted to put to Dwight when I asked for a meeting to discuss the leadership equation.

First was something that Dalton had raised with me a few days beforehand. A minister who enters the leadership race would have to immediately step down from Cabinet. If Dwight were to enter the race Dalton would lose his seasoned finance minister, right in the midst of truly difficult labour issues with the teachers and other public servants. Dalton said to me, "Selfishly, I hope Dwight doesn't run. I really need him where he is for the next few months."

Then there was the matter of whether Dwight was really committed to ten more years of hard labour as a politician. By then it was common knowledge that after so many years on the job Dwight was anxious for a life where he could work less and earn more. Finally, I wanted to be brutally honest in my personal assessment that, although Dwight would be the front-runner, it would be difficult for him to win the crown. And I did not want his political career to end by way of a second leadership loss. I made these points as tactfully as I could, wondering all the while whether I should have been minding my own business.

We talked some more about how to manage the last months of the McGuinty administration, and then it was over. I was touched by how sincerely he thanked me for my advice.

The leadership contest was shaping up nicely. We had seven really impressive candidates, all former McGuinty cabinet ministers: in alphabetical order, Eric Hoskins, Gerard Kennedy, Glen Murray, Sandra Pupatello, Charles Sousa, Harinder Takhar, and Kathleen Wynne.

Given my continuing responsibilities to the party, I agreed with the suggestion that we should create an informal election preparedness committee made up of some senior staff and party representatives (Dave Gene, Don Guy, Greg Wong, John Brodhead, Peter Curtis, Sophia Aggelonitis, Yasir Naqvi, Sharon Laredo, and myself), plus a representative from each leadership camp. The idea was to have everyone in the loop in case we found ourselves in an election campaign shortly after the new leader was chosen. I knew from experience that getting those wheels in motion could take quite some time. Yet there was a real possibility that our new leader might only have a few months before he or she was into a general election. It was none too early for a coalition team to be thinking about renting planes, buses, hotels, catering services, and technical vendors. We'd need a tour leader with a mandate to begin identifying, selecting, and training tour teams. We'd need to begin training party operatives — campaign managers, chief financial officers, and candidates. We'd need a policy creation process, based on the proposals made by the new leader and some of the other candidates. And so I thought it would be useful if we were all on the same page when it came to doing the things necessary for a snap election.

At least, that was the idea. And while it seemed like a good one at the time, the meetings were brutal. The tension between the representatives of the leadership candidates and the old McGuinty political operators was palpable. Moreover, their representatives were not able to come to any significant consensus. Some of them were on the verge of hostility toward me. Tom Allison, representing Kathleen Wynne, told us to mind our own business when it came to searching for new candidates. He told us if Wynne won, she'd be reviewing all the rules around candidate selection because she was concerned the central party had too much authority over the process and local riding associations had too little. I thought Tom's analysis was flawed. I've just never believed that a hundred people in one riding or another had all the knowledge and wisdom necessary to pick a candidate with no input from the central campaign.

As convention day approached, I actually revelled in my neutrality. As interim campaign and fundraising chair, I felt I needed to be unaligned, offering advice to all, but planting my flag with no one. I told anyone who cared that I was just keeping the seat warm until the new leader could pick his or her own replacement. And I was able to maintain that neutrality right up to convention day. Then, something happened that simply forced my hand.

Unlike most conventions, where candidate speeches are on a Friday night and the voting begins the following day, this convention scheduled both the speeches and voting all on Saturday, January 26, 2013. So the convention's agenda was compressed. That meant delegates wouldn't have a night to sleep on the speeches and consider their impact before voting. I had already come to a conclusion about two things well before the more than two thousand delegates gathered at the Gardens: first, who would win, and second, whom I was going to vote for. While I liked Eric Hoskins, Harinder Takhar, and Charles Sousa, I felt none was ready to lead our party. I kept waiting for Gerard Kennedy's campaign to take off, but in my view it never did. His challenge was to be more impressive than people expected, so much so that delegates would forget the fact that he had turned his back on the party five years earlier. But his speech and campaign were merely average. The choice for me was between the two female candidates. I simply felt that at the end of the day, Sandra Pupatello's being an "outsider" without a seat would render her unable to stop the hemorrhaging in the party. Nevertheless, I thought she'd win the convention. But I had decided even before arriving that Kathleen Wynne would get my vote. Eventually, she would get more than that.

Those of us who have been in and around politics for many years have seen our fair share of convention-day speeches. Frankly, not all of them are memorable. This day was different. Without question, Kathleen Wynne gave a leadership convention speech for the ages. It was brilliant. It challenged delegates to face down their own bigotry. Were they really prepared *not* to vote for the best candidate because she was a lesbian? Wynne reminded delegates there was a time in Ontario's not too distant past when having an Italian or Portuguese or South Asian family name rendered a candidate unsuitable for the leadership. She urged people to relegate those days to history's dustbin. The speech was breathtaking and historic.

Instantly and simultaneously, the two women sitting on either side of me told me to get off the fence and get involved. Those women were my wife, Kate, and my long-time adviser Sharon Laredo. Both insisted I use whatever sway I had to influence the outcome of this convention. "You can't just sit idly by," they told me.

In other words, help Wynne win.

I still didn't think it was appropriate for me to march over to Wynne's section of the arena, put on one of her buttons or scarves, and then thrust her hand into the air. But I needed to do something. As usual, Kate's advice was right. She persuaded me to do a scrum with some of the journalists on the floor of the convention.

"Kathleen Wynne has just given the best leadership convention speech I've ever heard," I told them. Then I saw long-time Liberal stalwart (and Wynne supporter) John Duffy prowling the halls. "John," I said, "I need you to spread the rumour that I've decided to support Kathleen." He didn't need to be told twice. Within five minutes, I got a call on my cellphone from TVO's Steve Paikin, who was anchoring the provincial broadcaster's coverage.

"I'm calling you to check out a rumour I just heard that you're no longer neutral and have decided to support Kathleen Wynne," Paikin said. "Is it true?"

"No," I assured him, "it's not true. I am not publicly supporting her. I simply said she gave the best speech of the day." Paikin didn't ask me whether I'd spread the rumour myself.

Much of the first ballot support was already locked in by virtue of the results of the delegate selection meetings, which had taken place earlier in the month. Those delegates were obligated to vote for the candidates on whose slates they got elected. But there were still hundreds of independent and ex officio delegates who were free agents and could vote for whomever they wanted after the speeches ended. Wynne's speech allowed her to take a disproportionately large chunk of that support. Heading into the first ballot, Pupatello had a forty-one vote lead over Wynne among already committed delegates. When the first ballot results, which then included the independent and ex officio delegates, were added and announced, Pupatello's lead shrank to just *two votes* over Wynne. With a race that close, the next move could very well decide the day.

Both Kate and Sharon immediately told me to go talk to Eric Hoskins, who had come last and was obliged to drop out of the contest. I waded my way through the packed floor of the hall and found myself face to face with Hoskins. "What do you think I should do?" he asked me. "You heard that speech, Eric," I told him. "You should go to Kathleen."

Unbeknownst to me, my moment with Hoskins was captured on camera. So what I'd hoped would be a quiet moment of influence turned into a big deal, seen by the entire television audience. Word spread quickly that my professed neutrality was now in the rear-view mirror.

In between the first and second ballot, I walked up to the upper level of the Gardens for some media interviews. There, I saw Deb Matthews. I didn't need to tell her what I had done. She knew. The resulting smile and enormous hug made my day.

While Hoskins's move to Wynne didn't ensure Kathleen's victory, it certainly set that result in motion. I laid low after my post-first-ballot intervention and didn't actively solicit anyone's vote. After the second ballot, Kennedy and Sousa dropped off and went to Wynne, while Takhar moved to Pupatello. Wynne won on the third ballot with 57 percent of the vote. In the end, it wasn't nearly as close as the first ballot results suggested it would be.

One of the major truisms of politics is that the amount of time you prevail in politics is inversely related to the rate at which you make enemies along the way. Fortunately, I had a good long run and didn't make too many enemies. But I made some. And on January 26, 2013, by helping Wynne win, I guaranteed that Sandra Pupatello would probably be my enemy for the rest of our lives. The next time we saw each other, she could barely contain herself.

"I lost because of you," she said bitterly.

I tried telling her that I seriously doubted that hundreds of delegates were sitting around waiting to hear what I would do before deciding how to cast their ballots. Still, I felt she had the right to feel offended that I'd broken my commitment to be neutral.

I saw Kathleen very briefly after her victory, told her I thought she'd given a brilliant speech, hugged her, and wished her well.

My next contact with Team Wynne came several days later. The premier-elect had decided to swear in her new Cabinet on February 11 and then follow it up a week after that with her first Speech from the Throne. Her first budget would come two months after that. In other words, there were some huge decisions to make and not much time to make them. So I accepted an invitation to join Wynne's transition team.

It did not feel comfortable. I quickly determined that the new premier should have her own advisers, unencumbered by the McGuinty players. It was time for us to leave the spotlight to others. The transition team was large and had plenty of luminaries. I suspect I had become overly accustomed to giving my advice directly to the boss and often seeing that advice acted upon. It was now time to bow out of the inner circle. I decided that I would not continue on the transition team. At the same time, I advised Tom Allison and former Liberal MPP Monique Smith that I was also stepping down as chair of the campaign and the Ontario Liberal Fund. I was now fully out of politics.

Two weeks later, Premier Wynne appointed Tim Murphy (former chief of staff to Prime Minister Paul Martin) and Deb Matthews (the health minister and deputy premier) to replace me as campaign co-chairs. The premier's press release noted: "[Greg Sorbara has] served as campaign chair for our last three election campaigns, and is owed a debt of gratitude from all of us. I sincerely thank Greg for everything he did for the last three campaigns."

Even as I was making my final political exit I resolved to maintain a strong working relationship with the new premier and her senior staff. Certainly there was some tension — to a person, the old McGuinty crew was not entirely welcome as any visible part of the new administration. I did not feel that this prohibition applied to me. I continued to meet from time to time with Kathleen and offer whatever advice seemed appropriate.

Thus, after the convention and before the new Cabinet was sworn in on February 11, 2013, I submitted my recommendations for the new Cabinet. I proposed Deb Matthews as an excellent minister of finance. Deb understood how government worked, what the major issues were, and, as health minister, was responsible for spending almost half the budget. She is a solid, empathetic politician who would have thrived at finance. Sadly, she declined.

Bob Chiarelli was doing a great job at infrastructure and transportation, and wanted to stay where he was. But he got moved to energy, which everyone knew would be a brutal job. The new minister would have to clean up the gas plant cancellation mess, deal with a public that was increasingly irate over rising electricity prices, and make some hard decisions about our plans to bring more green energy into the province's mix. Conversely, Glen Murray took over Chiarelli's old job; soon his penchant for seizing the issue occasionally got him into trouble, particularly on the Scarborough subway file. He'd have been a better choice, I thought, at community and social services, where his powerful empathy for the less well-off would have been an asset.

I thought the new Cabinet needed to be younger and more activist, so I was disappointed to see seventy-two-year-old Mario Sergio in, and Steven Del Duca, a guy three decades younger, out. I was happy to see Brad Duguid and Yasir Naqvi in, but was perplexed to see seventy-year-old John Gerretsen in as attorney general, especially since it was pretty much a given that he wouldn't be running again. It broke my heart to see Laurel Broten, a good lawyer, marginalized at intergovernmental affairs rather than appointed as just the second female attorney general in Ontario history. I suspect the premier needed to show the teachers' unions that she was punishing the former minister of education for daring to claw back some of their sick days. What a statement it would have made to have a female premier, a female deputy premier, a female finance minister, a female attorney general, and a female education minister. I thought it was a missed opportunity. Five months later, Broten quit politics altogether and moved to Halifax.

Early on, my most controversial recommendation was to bury the hatchet with Sandra Pupatello and invite her to become finance minister. Bringing the two finalists together in Cabinet would have been a stellar move. I talked to the premier's deputy chief of staff, Tom Allison, about it and he agreed to allow me to broach the idea with Sandra. I loved everything about the idea. It would have united the two main camps of the leadership race and their combatants. Sandra would have been a fantastic finance minister. From her time as economic development minister, she understood all the issues so well.

I also pointed to the example from American politics where President Barack Obama had appointed his chief opponent, Hillary Clinton, to be his secretary of state. In that case the move worked brilliantly, and the former rivals became wonderful partners in the Obama administration.

I called Sandra and made all those points and more. I reminded her that one of the greatest first minister–finance minister partnerships in Canadian history was between Jean Chrétien and Paul Martin, who certainly didn't love each other but worked extremely well together for several years. I pointed out that Hillary Clinton was now the odds-on favourite to replace Obama as the Democratic Party's standard-bearer in 2016, and that if Premier Wynne faltered, Sandra would still be a decade younger and perfectly positioned to assume the crown. "Sandra," I told her, "that might not have been your last leadership convention. Think about this."

Unfortunately, the idea just never got any traction among the two protagonists. Kathleen's relationship with Sandra was cool. And when I talked to Sandra on the phone about the idea, she spent forty-five minutes tearing a strip off me like no one ever had before. She was still furious at me and pretty much everyone else, leading me to conclude this was just never going to happen.

"It's your fault she's there and I'm here," Sandra told me. There was just a thick sheen of bitterness I couldn't penetrate. I called Tom Allison with the bad news. "Sorry, Tom," I said. "I was convinced of the wisdom of the idea, but there's just no hope."

The Wynne Cabinet was sworn into office on February 11, 2013. I wasn't able to be there, but within a week the new premier and I met.

"The people of Ontario need you to be in government for at least a year, or a year and a half," I told her. "You have to establish your own style. Govern well, and don't go to the polls quickly."

Certainly there were those in the inner circle who were advising the new premier to call a snap election. The minority parliament had become dysfunctional, they argued, and a quick election would give Premier Wynne her own mandate and relegate to the past the litany of controversies that she had inherited from her predecessor — in particular, the gas plant issues. However, the majority view was to attempt to make the minority parliament work. Indeed, that was Wynne's personal preference and what she considered her mandate to be from the delegates who elected her to the premiership.

At her first major speech to the province, delivered at the March 20, 2013, Heritage Dinner, she made an eloquent case for co-operation with the opposition parties. The only significant hurdle would be passage of the new government's first budget, to be delivered by Finance Minister Sousa later in the spring. While the budget did ultimately pass, the atmosphere in parliament continued to deteriorate. For me, the low point arrived when PC leader Hudak publicly accused Wynne of conspiring with others to delete emails relating to the gas plant controversy. An exasperated Wynne responded with a suit for libel against Hudak. It was the right response and about the only arrow left in the premier's quiver.

From my perspective, Wynne was spending far too little time defining a new and more positive agenda, one that used the many achievements of the McGuinty era as a base for new initiatives that would capture the imagination of a skeptical population.

By January 2014, I had become so concerned by the government's lack of progress and the beating it was taking from all sides that I decided to take a dramatic proposal to the premier and her senior advisers. I suggested the premier begin the winter session of parliament with a kind of "State of the Province" address in the legislature, at the end of which she would announce her intention to introduce a bill to set the date for the next election for June 19, 2014. The speech, I argued, would make the point that it was urgent that parliament get on with the province's business and pass the 2014 Budget in an atmosphere not so politically charged — but that thereafter it would be appropriate for the electors to have their say. I surmised that voters had become accustomed to fixed election dates, that the tedious drama about how long the government could survive needed to end, and that as a matter of principle it should be up to parliament and not the Cabinet to decide on the timing of elections. Most important, taking this position would dispel any suggestion that Premier Wynne feared an election.

While I sensed some initial interest, my scheme was soon rejected and the political environment continued to degenerate. Then things began to change for the better.

From conversations with a number of people, including David Herle, the party's campaign director, and Pat Sorbara, the campaign manager, it became clear to me that Ontario Liberals were diligently preparing for a general election in mid-June in any event. That suited me just fine. There was nothing further that the fractured minority parliament could accomplish. And as a purely practical matter, June 2014 was the only available window for an Ontario election. The fall of 2014 would be off limits because the province would be involved in municipal elections from September to the end of October. December is uniformly considered inappropriate for electioneering, and from January 1, 2015, onward the preoccupation across Canada would be the federal election set for October 2015. The provincial party would have no appetite for competing with federal Liberals in 2015 for the money and the volunteers needed to run a competent campaign.

The only remaining question was how to bring an end to a dysfunctional parliament. As it turned out, the key to the solution was the budget that Charles Sousa was proposing to present on May 1, 2014, and the inexplicable misstep that NDP leader Andrea Horwath took the next day.

Sousa's budget was as uncompromising in its appeal to the centre and centre-left of the political spectrum as any I had ever seen. Under normal circumstances it would have been unthinkable for the NDP to reject this kind of budget. Wynne, with uncharacteristic determination, made it clear that either Horwath would announce her acceptance of the budget or Wynne would seek dissolution of parliament from Lieutenant-Governor David Onley. The bait was set and Horwath bit. She announced her party would not support the budget under any circumstances, because the Wynne government could not be trusted to deliver on what the budget promised. Parliament was dissolved on May 2, and Ontarians would be going to the polls on June 12.

As the campaign began it was anyone's guess as to what the final outcome would be. Voters across the province were in a foul mood. More than one proposed that a candidate named *"None of the Above"* be added to the every ballot in the province. Initial polling added no real insight into which party might prevail. Many suggested that Ontario would get yet another minority parliament, a result that would lead to more years of political bickering.

The Liberal campaign got off to a healthy start. It was obvious from day one that the Liberals had been fully prepared for a June campaign and were determined to win. During the previous six months they had been concerned about two things: the possibility of a rising tide for the NDP (which could have the effect of electing Tories in many rural ridings) and a Progressive Conservative campaign that was rooted exclusively on a growing appetite for a change at Queen's Park. Their concerns proved to be unfounded.

Through six weeks of the campaign the NDP effort never really got off the ground. It was one of the great ironies of Campaign 2014 that the party that had forced the election was the one party that was not at all prepared to contest it. The NDP had not nominated a full slate of candidates; early on there was no party platform; even technical issues like tour buses and a tour agenda did not seem to be ready. Then it got worse. As the Horwath platform unfolded, it appeared she was attempting to do the impossible — abandon the traditional core support of her party in the hope of creating a new base to the centre and centre-right of the political spectrum. That violated the primary rule of campaign preparation — that first you do what is necessary and appropriate to solidify your base and then you work out strategies to expand to the right or left, depending on circumstances. In the middle of the campaign, a group of some thirty-four prominent members of Horwath's party issued an open letter decrying her abandonment of what they considered sacred social democratic principles. Thereafter, it appeared to many that Horwath was simply going through the motions.

Unlike Horwath, Tim Hudak was fully prepared for the campaign, with pamphlets printed and buses wrapped. Perhaps he was too ready. Most Liberals feared that a kinder, gentler, more centrist Hudak might win the support of voters who simply felt it was time for a change. Instead, Hudak moved his party even farther to the right and developed a platform based on the notion that the sky was falling in Ontario and we all ought to be running for our lives. At the core of the Hudak campaign was his Million Jobs Plan to be accompanied by severe cuts in government spending. As part of the plan, Hudak announced early on that if elected he would proceed to fire one hundred thousand public servants. Instantly, a million Ontarians who work at one level or another in the broader public sector began to worry about losing their jobs. Neither they nor their families would be voting for the Tories. It got worse. Mid-campaign, a group of economists who had analyzed the Million Jobs Plan reported the Tories had made an obvious mathematical error in their calculations. Suddenly, the Tory plan appeared to be full of holes.

In my experience, the key to winning a general election is credibility. The leader and the party that appear most credible through all the surrounding campaign noise will almost always prevail. On that scale, Kathleen Wynne outran her two opponents by a country mile. Most voters, even those who were determined not to vote Liberal, saw her as competent, credible, sincere, and determined. They found her to be energetic and likeable despite the mud slung her way every day of the campaign.

Certainly there were hiccups. Wynne did not do well in the leaders' debate. She spent far too much time on the defensive, apologizing far too often for things that were never her responsibility. Many of us worried the tide would turn again because of the debate. By election day, no one I knew was willing to bet the family farm on what the result might be. And yet within an hour of the close of voting the Liberals had won with a comfortable majority. The final result was fifty-eight seats for the Liberals, twenty-eight for the PCs, and twenty-one for the NDP. We ought not to have been surprised. It should have been obvious that, given the options, Ontarians would choose the stability and credibility that Wynne and the Liberals offered to Ontario.

The Liberals won because, in the main, voters preferred Kathleen Wynne to Tim Hudak or Andrea Horwath. They won because, in the main, voters preferred a moderate, centrist government to one that hoped to emulate the American Tea Party agenda. But there was another important factor. While credibility is extremely important, winning campaigns are ones that are well organized on the ground. As campaign manager, Pat Sorbara can take the lion's share of the credit for a "ground war" that was as good as any in recent history. Unlike this Sorbara, Pat has never had an appetite for the spotlight. Yet, in the opinion of many, she was the shining star of Wynne's victory.

Campaign 2014 was an entirely new experience for me. After fourteen years in the Liberal trenches I played absolutely no role in the election. Several days before the campaign began, an announcement was made that I would be succeeding the legendary Roy McMurtry as the new Chancellor of York University. It is customary and appropriate that university chancellors abstain from partisan politics. For me that meant no more fundraising, no more endorsements, no more door-knocking, no more strategy sessions, no more political cheerleading of any kind. My very final exit from politics became in fact the beginning of a wonderful new step in my life's journey — promoting the importance of post-secondary education for one university in particular and for the province in general. It is work that I will relish.

13

What's Ahead

If one ignores a few years on the sidelines, I ended up spending almost three decades in the ebb and flow of electoral politics. Often I view my experience as an accidental career. There was never any grand design, nor any intense ambition to become a political celebrity.

Now, as I look back, I have come to realize that what inspired those years was a singular preoccupation with the state of the province and the nation and with what one could and could not do to strengthen the fabric that weaves us together as a Canadian community.

Circumstances led me to the theatre of provincial politics in Ontario. It was a stage that I thoroughly enjoyed. Now my role as an active Ontario Liberal Party lieutenant has come to end. Still, I continue to think about — and fret about — where we go from here, what steps we might take, both large and small, to bring about a fairer, more equitable society and improve the collective lot of the 35 million people for whom this massive and majestic stretch of land is home.

In that regard I am decidedly a Wilfrid Laurier Liberal. It was Laurier who in 1877 famously said: "I am a Liberal. I am one of these who think that everywhere, in human things, there are abuses to be reformed, new horizons to be opened up, and new forces to be developed."

Where are those abuses that need our attention today? U.S. president Barack Obama has made it clear that, in his view, income inequality, the growing gap in American society, is the most important issue of our time. It is most certainly the greatest threat to maintaining a cohesive society in the United States.

But not just in the United States. Recently, the International Monetary Fund, the world's top economic institution, sounded the alarm about the growing gap between rich and poor worldwide. It warned that rising income inequality is stunting global economic growth and contributing to further political instability. The Fund set out a variety of tax policy reforms to begin to address the issue.

The case has recently been made by American author Robert Reich, the former secretary of labour in the Clinton administration. In his book *Aftershock* he points out that in the late 1970s the top 1 percent of income earners took home less than 8 percent of America's total income. By Bill Clinton's first election in 1992, the take had jumped to 13 percent of total income. Today, the top 1 percent captures nearly *a quarter* of all Americans' income.

The statistics in Canada are not so stark, but the trends here should be of equal concern. The earning capacity of the great Canadian middle class has been stagnant for a long time, while the affluence of our economic elites continues to grow at a rapid rate. And there appears to be nothing on the national agenda to counteract that trend.

We have not had a significant re-examination of our system of taxation and wealth distribution since the Carter Commission established by the Diefenbaker administration over fifty years ago. Since then, the Canadian economy has been totally transformed. Surely it is time now for a comprehensive re-examination of the tools that regulate the creation of wealth and its distribution, and the capacity to fund public enterprise, from income support to infrastructure development.

In my view, the best evidence that this work is long overdue is the state of finances of every Canadian government. Instead of designing revenue policies that match the need for funding public services, governments simply increase the burden of deficits that future generations will have to contend with.

The notion of income support for those in need has been deeply ingrained in Canadian society for decades. That commitment has resulted in a cornucopia of programs at all levels of government. The list is long:

Employment Insurance, Canada Pension Plan, Old Age Security, Guaranteed Income Supplement, Disability Pensions, and Workers' Compensation, provincial and municipal welfare programs, federal and provincial child benefit programs, property tax rebates, rent supplements, tuition assistance. The list goes on until all else fails — and then there are food banks.

All of these programs share a single common objective, to provide income support for those who, for one reason or another, no longer have the capacity to make it on their own. The reality is that administering so many different programs carries a very high cost for public administration. Tens of thousands of bureaucrats work tirelessly at all levels of government designing, administering, and adjudicating these programs to support those in need.

Surely there is a better way and one that is more efficient. My notion of a better and more efficient system would be a comprehensive Canadian Income Security System, or CISS, administered by the national government in Ottawa. Municipalities have no business being in the welfare business, and the capacity of provinces to provide adequate levels of support varies across the country. Only the federal government has the capacity to generate the revenues and administer the system right across the country to respond to the needs in every region in a fair and substantive way.

The reform of the taxation and income support is but one area where a truly inspired national government could strengthen the fibres that weave us together as a nation.

The sad reality of the current Conservative government in Ottawa is its utter absence of any agenda that strengthens the bonds of Canadian society. Indeed, it seems a matter of pride for that government to avoid such initiatives at all costs. This stands in sharp contrast to an enviable tradition of Canadian prime ministers from Macdonald to Martin who took it as their mission to further unite a small population across a vast land. Macdonald's railroad, Laurier's modernization of government, King's war efforts and employment insurance, Diefenbaker's Bill of Rights, Pearson's Medicare and Canada Pension Plan, Trudeau's Charter of Rights, Mulroney's free trade agreements and tax reforms, and Chrétien's and Martin's fiscal reforms are just a few of the ways our prime ministers have responded to this unifying mission.

Harper, through eight years, has shown little interest in such initiatives other than trying to glamorize Canadian war efforts. In response to issues of mental health, drug dependence, poverty, and the alienation of Native communities, his response has been to build larger prisons and lock up more and more people for longer and longer periods of time.

On the question of a Canadian national agenda, it is instructive indeed that Prime Minister Harper has made it a matter of pride to discontinue the First Ministers' Conference forum. That forum, last used by Paul Martin, was the only context where all Canadian governments had a regular opportunity to analyze, discuss, and debate issues that could strengthen the bonds of Canadian society.

It is trite to say that if we are not talking together there is nothing that we are going to achieve together. That is the reality today in Canada, where every province and territory is on its own, region is pitted against region on a variety of economic issues, and little is done to help us share our common Canadian citizenship.

For Ontario this is a strange new world.

Historically, Ontario premiers had a sixth sense for issues of national unity. In 1967, John Robarts brought the country together with the Confederation of Tomorrow Conference; Bill Davis worked alongside Pierre Trudeau to repatriate the Canadian Constitution; David Peterson tried desperately to confirm a national consensus within the Meech Lake Accord; Bob Rae helped craft the Charlottetown Accord; and Dalton McGuinty collaborated with Paul Martin to secure a national health-care accord in 2004. Once the federal Conservatives came to power, the meetings of First Ministers were simply cancelled. The next government in Ottawa should make them a regular component of the nation's agenda.

A new national government should also end the tedious debate on Senate reform by voluntarily transferring the Senate appointment process out of the political hands of the prime minister and changing the rules such that the Senate becomes a non-partisan body populated by 104 independent members.

The next federal government should also create a department of urban affairs and through it invest much more in the construction of urban infrastructure. A significant majority of Canadians now live in large cities. The needs of those cities need to become a priority.

And finally there is the matter of Canada's foreign policy. The reorientation of that policy toward making our country a more bellicose ally of those who believe there is only black and white is for me a matter of great sadness. In this area I am decidedly a Pearsonian liberal. I believe that Lester Pearson's efforts at casting Canada as an honest broker and peace-keeper in world affairs gave rise to a level of global respect that was unprecedented for such a small nation. In this arena we need to return to Pearsonian principles.

A good deal of Ontario's future prospects will depend on how the national agenda plays out over the next decade. After all, we are but one province in a federal state that must compete within a global economy.

A recent report from my former ministry — the twenty-year outlook for Ontario's economy — suggested rather sluggish growth over the period and an increasing demand on public services, notably health care, to serve the needs of an aging population.

As for me, I do not think that we need simply accept the notion that Ontario's future will be decidedly cooler than its past. There are a number of things that should be included in the province's agenda to strengthen our prospects.

Invariably, the number one item on the agenda is the economy, including productivity growth, job creation, new business development, and higher real wages.

Among the things that hold promise is the potential for Ontario's far north, including the development of the so-called Ring of Fire, five hundred kilometres northeast of Thunder Bay. The Ring holds billions of dollars worth of chromite under the earth's surface; it represents massive economic potential for Ontario. But the political, environmental, and societal challenges are enormous. Stephen Harper, who has been so helpful in developing Alberta's oil patch, has been less than energetic when it comes to the Ring of Fire. Would that he cared as much about developing those natural resources as he does about pushing the Keystone XL pipeline. A co-ordinated national effort in Ontario's far north could change the lives of indigenous Ontarians, and of people in the rest of the province, too.

Typically, the average Ontarian does not see the province as an exporting economy. For that reason, perhaps, the provincial government has never put a great deal of independent effort into expanding the province's capacity to enhance trade with emerging economies. That needs to change. The McGuinty government made a short-lived effort in this area after the 2007 election, when it created a ministry of international trade and made Sandra Pupatello the minister in charge. But there was little real commitment to make trade a priority, and few real resources were directed to creating an Ontario presence in targeted markets. The ministry did not last long and the initiative was abandoned. In my view, the Pan Am games to be hosted by Toronto in June 2015 represent an obvious opportunity to begin to pursue new economic relations, and greater trade, with many of the nations that will come to play in Ontario at that time.

We also need to get serious about strengthening the economies in small-city Ontario. The magnetic pull of the Greater Toronto Area ensures a dynamic economy for our capital city. But what about the rest of the province? What about the Windsors, the Londons, the Hamiltons, the Kingstons, the North Bays, or the Sault Ste. Maries? Back in the 1980s, the Peterson government moved several ministries out of Toronto to smaller cities, to give them hundreds of permanent, decent-paying jobs. Those jobs became part of the backbone of those cities' economies. The Ontario Lottery and Gaming Commission moved to Sault Ste. Marie. The agriculture ministry moved to Guelph. The ministry of transportation moved to St. Catharines. Those were effective initiatives to diversify those economies. It's time to rethink what this generation can do to bring strength to small cities and more rural communities.

One of the things I wanted to do when I was still in government was move the Workplace Safety and Insurance Board head office to Hamilton. I pointed out that Hamilton was the largest city in the province without a provincial head office. The WSIB would be a strong candidate. Hamilton has had a proud blue-collar reputation, and the Hamilton Workers' Occupational Health and Safety Centre was already established there. I had some talks with WSIB head Steve Mahoney and then with Hamilton mayor Fred Eisenberger. Steel-making jobs at Stelco and Dofasco were disappearing by the thousands, and I thought that injecting Hamilton with hundreds of permanent, well-paid jobs would help. But there just wasn't much appetite for my idea.

We need to change how we support public services as well. It is high time, for example, to begin designing a strategy to eliminate tuition at the undergraduate level of post-secondary education. There was a time when basic education meant completing grade 8. Decades later the basic requirement was the completion of one high school program or another. Today there are ever fewer prospects for those who have not completed a post-secondary program or apprenticeship prior to entering the workforce. Public education should now include full tuition support through the undergraduate post-secondary years.

It may take as many as ten years or more to fully implement a tuition-free undergraduate system. There are a host of challenging issues to examine and resolve. That is no excuse, however, not to make the political commitment and begin the design work.

Then there is the issue of our existing public education system and what the future holds for it. For me the big issue is whether it continues to be enlightened public policy to fund two independent parallel systems, one public and one for Ontario's large Catholic population. I am fully aware of the all the constitutional issues and historical commitments; in my first year in Cabinet, the Peterson government legislated full funding for the Catholic system. I have no illusions about how toxic a political issue this is: I grew up in the Catholic tradition; at sixteen I was determined to become a Catholic priest.

Despite all that, I believe it is time now for Ontario to move to one public education system for all. This is not to say that the Catholic system has not served us well. It has. But this is not the Ontario of 1867 when the Protestant majority agreed to accommodate Catholics with "separate schools" as much to keep the Catholic kids away from their own children as to make concessions for a greater common goal.

The Ontario of today is a secular society that is a welcome home to every religion in the world. It is our strong suit, an operational example of how a pluralist multicultural jurisdiction can and should work.

Special accommodation for one religion and one religion only no longer seems appropriate to our circumstances.

Would this be a difficult challenge? Of course it would. But this very reform has been implemented elsewhere in Canada and now needs to be addressed here at home.

It seems as though the list of urgent issues that confronts us never gets shorter. However, for me, the curtain is coming down, and it is my turn to leave the stage. I leave with a sense of hope that our democracy will develop new strength and engender new passion for the challenges ahead.

This can only happen if the great majority of Ontarians renew their collective belief in and commitment to how we govern ourselves. In the end it is the energy and ambition of 13 million Ontarians, working through our democratic system, that will ensure the prosperity of our province into the future.

Appendix 1

WHO DOES THE REAL WORK?

It is the case in so many aspects of our media-dominated, personality-obsessed culture that the spotlight tends to shine on one person, even when that one person merely represents a much larger supporting cast. Ironically, without that supporting cast, which often labours in obscurity, the person who is front and centre would not be able to achieve anything remotely resembling the triumph for which the media give this one person the credit.

In that regard, perhaps the single most bang-on piece of advice I got on this score came from the first premier I served, David Peterson. Shortly after I was elected in 1985, I found myself in a quiet moment with the premier, who had already been an MPP for ten years. He was trying to give me a greater understanding of the role of elected politician I had just assumed.

"Greg, here's what's going to happen to you one day," he began. "You'll be walking down the street, minding your own business, when you'll be stopped by a complete stranger. That person will say, 'Greg Sorbara, I can't tell you how grateful I am to you. You turned my life around and I'll never forget you.'

"You won't know who that person is," Peterson continued. "You won't know what they're talking about. But here's what you'll know: someone in your office resolved a personal crisis in the life of that person."

Nearly three decades after that conversation, I can confirm that the former premier was spot on. The scene he described played itself out numerous times in my life, and it happened because I was fortunate enough to surround myself with great people, whose job it was in part to make me look good. And they did.

Why does someone sign on for a job where he or she will do all the work, but someone else will get all the glory? I've thought about this question a lot over the years and have concluded that the human race is made up of all varieties of people. For some, giving a speech to a roomful of people generates a fear worse than death. Politicians aren't part of that group. We love to meet people and try to win them over. It's what we do. But there are also extremely talented people who are drawn to politics because they love dealing with public policy issues but have absolutely no appetite for the spotlight.

Whether you're the president of the United States of America or the reeve of Billings Township on Manitoulin Island in Ontario, whether it's your first moment in public life or your last, it is absolutely true that success, or failure, for that matter, happens because of the team. It's rarely portrayed that way in the popular press. But that is the way it is.

I've had the pleasure of having led many different teams during my quarter century in politics, everything from a constituency association responsible for just one of 107 ridings to a general election team responsible for putting our best foot forward across the entire province. I can still clearly recall the very first people representing the Liberal Party of Ontario that I ever met. In the winter of 1984, I had a conversation with a staffer at Queen's Park named Loretta Serafini, who urged me to become a candidate. Her ally was a local Vaughan councillor named Nick DiGiovanni. Then Bruce Walkinshaw, president of the York North Provincial Liberal Riding Association, got on board. Bruce had toiled in the political wilderness for years in what seemed like a hopeless mission — winning the riding for a Liberal candidate. I gave my first speech at my nominating meeting in York Region's King City in front of twenty-seven people. Twenty-five of them were directly related to me. The speech was stilted and uninspiring, but it was a start.

Shortly thereafter, the campaign began, and I was shocked at the number of people who kept coming out, day after day, to volunteer. I was a complete unknown in the riding and assumed getting people to sign on and help would be an impossible task. And yet there they were. Eventually twenty to thirty hardy souls joined our daily crusade.

At first it was a complete mystery to me as to why these folks would want to take time out of their lives to join the team. Eventually I came to realize some were there out of a sense of civic duty to a party they loved, regardless of who was the candidate. Others knew me and thought it would be an exciting but brief adventure to join an election campaign. In that category, I think of people such as Adrianna Delfino, who was participating in an election for the first time. After I won in 1985 and found myself with two Cabinet jobs, I suggested to Adrianna that, since I needed a scheduling assistant, she might be interested in doing the job. I assured her it would only take two to three days a week of her time. She agreed.

We both quickly discovered there's no one in a minister's office that's busier than the scheduling assistant. And more often than not, her most important skill was figuring out how, in the nicest way possible, to tell people, No I'm sorry, you can't see the minister.

Some of the other people I brought on board in that first minister's office included a young man who had lobbied on behalf of the Ontario Federation of Students. His name was Bob Richardson. He became my legislative adviser, and his job was to open doors to the post-secondary sector. Barb Sulzenko became my executive assistant and was instrumental in bringing forward the groundbreaking Futures program.

Members of the legislature are elected to take care of a constituency, but a great staff doing great work for the MPP's constituents is essential for the politician's success. An MPP's constituency staff deals with myriad problems that individuals have with an increasingly complex provincial government. In fact, I shouldn't limit it to just the provincial government, since members of the public approach us on issues that other governments are actually tasked to deal with. The job of the MPP and his or her staff is simple: find a solution to that constituent's problem. Oftentimes, however, it can be maddeningly complicated. One moment, a staffer can be trying to secure a pension from the Workplace Safety and Insurance Board for an injured worker. The next moment, a single mother will plead her case for social assistance, without which she can't pay her rent. As MPPs, we get the credit for successfully resolving these problems. But it's our staffers who really make the trains run on time.

Because my first constituency was so big, I actually had three offices in the riding. Grace Isgro ran the office in Woodbridge. Bunny Godman did the same in Aurora. There was a third office in Whitchurch-Stouffville. After the 1987 election campaign, Helen Poulis joined my team. She ended up staying with me to the very end in 2012. She answered phones, opened files for constituents, and kept me in touch with all the gossip around the riding. Her dedication to my success as a politician was as deep as that of anyone I've ever encountered in public life. Unprompted, she even kept a historical record of my journey by way of a scrapbook of newspaper clippings.

Wendy Ground had a long history at Queen's Park and came to work for me in 2002. During the 2003 election campaign she took a leave to run my Aurora campaign office. The only space available on Main Street was one with no hydro power. So Wendy took it upon herself to buy generators, batteries, and lanterns to the keep the lights on.

Rose Vecchiarelli was another of the truly great constituency office workers. I actually inherited Rose. She was working at Queen's Park for another Liberal MPP named Ray Haggerty. When Ray retired in 1990, I snagged Rose. There hasn't been an MPP who was ever better served by a constituency office worker than Rose. She spent all day solving problems for constituents. Then, in the evening, she would work for the provincial riding association, helping to organize fundraisers or community events. For example, when a spring festival in Aurora required setting up a booth for the local MPP, it was Rose and her team that did all the work to make that happen. My job was to arrive at 2:00 p.m. and shake hands with people till 4:30. I often felt so humbled to be associated with so many people who did so much on my behalf. I didn't feel worthy of so much dedication.

It's remarkable how the role of the constituency office has developed over time. Robert Nixon tells the story of what Premier Leslie Frost had told him when he was first elected in 1963: "You've been elected to a seat in the Ontario legislature and that's what you're going to get." By that Frost meant no staff, no office, not even a telephone. Back in those days, the members had to use a pay phone situated outside the legislative chamber. But things evolved. Frost's successor, John Robarts, gave a little bit of budget to members so they could hold "clinics" on the weekend and see constituents. Today, MPPs are each given a quarter of a million dollars to rent a constituency office and staff it with two to three full-time employees and volunteers.

Unlike the system in the United States, no one in Ontario gets to be a cabinet minister until he or she is first elected in the local constituency. I've been fortunate enough to have had that happen seven times. When I returned to politics in a 2001 by-election, I actually hadn't sought elective office since the 1990 election. I was concerned as to whether I could put the team back together again after more than a decade on the sidelines. And the by-election was a crucial test not only for me, but for Dalton McGuinty's leadership. It's not an exaggeration to say that if I, as president of the Liberal Party, had lost that by-election, it could have dealt a fatal blow to the Liberal leader's prospects.

But remarkably, sometimes as many as a hundred volunteers showed up in the office and on the streets of Vaughan-King-Aurora. It was truly a magnificent crew of volunteers and Queen's Park staffers. No one worked harder than Giovanni Di Pierdomenico. Giovanni is eighty-four years old now. He's a retired custodial manager with the Peel Region District School Board who was one of the most aggressive and energetic campaigners I ever saw. He was on the streets every day, badgering his fellow Italian-Canadians to "vote for Sorbara." Even the younger campaign workers couldn't match his enthusiasm.

When it comes to campaigning, one of the things that never ceases to amaze me is how the sign crews do their thing. I'm just a little bit ashamed to admit this, but in seven election campaigns I have never actually put a sign into someone's front lawn, except for a photo-op. It is a shocking thing to see an election called, and then within days drive through one's riding to see thousands upon thousands of signs on people's front lawns. Steven Del Duca, my one-time campaign manager and executive assistant who succeeded me as the MPP for Vaughan, once told me he wanted to double our order for signs. I told him he was crazy. He insisted he wasn't. "I know Vaughan-King-Aurora," he said. "People here like to proclaim who they're for." Sure enough, we put up ten thousand signs during that campaign. And amazingly enough, within three days of the campaign's end the signs were all down and collected. It's just pure dedication.

In 2003, a tall young man named Lorenzo Catuzza volunteered for my campaign in Vaughan-King-Aurora. He'd just completed a university degree in English and philosophy, which I thought was a great background for a life in politics. Lorenzo worked on my campaign every day. After its successful conclusion, I asked him if he would consider working for me. He did and stayed through right to the end of my career, working on as wide a variety of assignments as anyone. When the government decided to build a new provincial hospital in Vaughan, I got a huge amount of the credit. But Lorenzo and I know that he did much of the leg work. He advised me on how to wage the battles. He nagged the right ministry of health and long term care officials to move them to a positive decision. We'll start building the Mackenzie Vaughan Hospital in 2015 thanks to Lorenzo. His commitment to the Vaughan community now has him contesting a seat on local council.

I also have fond memories of a campaign team that worked so well together to win three elections for Dalton McGuinty at the dawn of the twenty-first century. Those team members included Don Guy, the campaign director, who made it a matter of religion never to have his name or picture appear in a newspaper article. I was surprised after our 2003 election victory to see a reference to my name as "the architect of the Liberal victory." Sure, it was flattering, but it didn't acknowledge the extent of the team, which, besides Don, included Dave Gene, the campaign manager; Gerald Butts, who led our policy development; and Dave Pryce, the executive director of the party. Nor did it acknowledge the crucial communications team, which included Matt Maychak, Sheila James, Chris Morley, and Tracey Sobers.

As a matter of law, a provincial general election is the responsibility of the Ontario Liberal Party (OLP). I served as OLP president from November 1999 until February 2004. During that time I had an all-star crew of OLP executive council members, including Kim Donaldson, executive vice-president, and Peter Wilkinson, the party's treasurer. The 2003 campaign was the first in which we used a new official — the OLP nominations commissioner. Our first nominations commissioner was Rod MacDonald. Rod had a long history at Queen's Park, going back to Murray Elston's time in government. It was Rod's job to ensure that the party's interests were well represented in nomination meetings across Ontario.

206 · GREG SORBARA

During an election campaign the leader is on television every day. But that obscures the fact that there is also an army of thirty to forty people who work day and night at Liberal headquarters at 10 St. Mary Street in downtown Toronto, crammed into very modest and limited quarters. There is nothing to compare with the intense dedication of those who populate a campaign headquarters during the twenty-eight-day marathon that is a provincial election. Not too far down the road you would find Greg Wong's army, burning the midnight oil at 243 College Street, raising money for the campaign. During the 2003 election campaign, Phil Olsson, a Bay Street financier, led the Ontario Liberal Fund, ably assisted by Henry Pankratz. He was succeeded by one of Ontario's best builders, who has turned his company into a global player in construction: Geoff Smith of Ellis Don. I was constantly in awe of Geoff, who ran a very large business and yet volunteered so much of his time to raise money for our provincial party. Perhaps it was in his blood. Thirty years earlier, his father Don Smith was president of the party, and his mother, Joan Smith, was one of David Peterson's cabinet ministers.

Of course, during campaigns or a blitz to sell out the Heritage Dinner, the OLF office would have as many as a dozen volunteers working the phones. I think of stalwarts like Gary Singh who never said no to our request for help raising money or organizing rallies. And he rallied relentlessly at us about reflecting the grand diversity of Ontario's citizenry.

As wonderful as my memories are of working with some truly fine people in my constituency offices and for the party, I think the most impressive staff we ever assembled was during my years as minister of finance. By the time I was sworn in, I had enough experience to know that my success would depend on the staff I put together for that job. As was the case in 1985, the first task was to pick a chief of staff. Peter Wilkinson and I had worked together for the party, I as president and he as treasurer. Peter was working in a well-paying senior executive position for the Canadian Institute of Chartered Accountants. My long-time adviser Sharon Laredo planted the seed in my head that Peter was our man. To my delight, he answered the call, and together we assembled what I'll immodestly call the best political staff any minister ever had at Queen's Park. Mark Stabile, the youngest ever economics professor at the University of Toronto, joined us after a recommendation from Gerald

Butts. I called Karim Bardeesy, who had worked for Sean Conway in opposition. "Karim," I said, "I'm not asking you to come work with me in finance, I'm *telling* you. You have to do this and I won't take no for an answer." Fortunately, I didn't have to. Karim joined the team as my legislative assistant and eventually worked his way up to Premier Dalton McGuinty's senior policy adviser.

We snagged two great staffers out of the ministry of finance bureaucracy: Daniel Malik and Christine Allenby. I was captivated by Daniel's quirkiness and intensity. He had a huge appetite for taking on more and more files. Christine developed a passion for the job and combined that with her dedication to baseball, which she played almost every night of the summer. When our time together was done she found a job in Premier McGuinty's office.

Director of communications is one of the toughest jobs in finance, and Diane Flanagan was one of our best finds. She had been a staffer for former Liberal MPP Carman McClelland in the 1980s and then worked for the Bank of Nova Scotia. She knew politics. She knew banking too, and she knew communications. Among her many strong suits was her ability to get me to hold my tongue.

Eglinton-Lawrence MPP Mike Colle was my parliamentary assistant. Arthur Lofsky was his executive assistant. When Mike was promoted to Cabinet as minister of citizenship and immigration, we convinced Arthur to stick around and continue to help us. He managed to combine a talent for public policy and Liberal Party politics in a way few others would. He solved huge political problems for us, including reducing auto insurance premiums, and almost single-handedly revised the property tax system in Ontario. I got the credit. Both Arthur and I know he did the lion's share of the work.

The nature of politics being what it is, people come and go quite frequently. When we lost Peter to Dalton McGuinty's office as the premier's chief of staff, Diane Flanagan ably filled his shoes. Sean Hamilton became communications director. Michael Arbour became part of Sean's team.

Sean Mullin served as a junior policy staffer in my office. By 2011 he was the senior guy on financial matters in Dalton McGuinty's office.

Other than Sharon Laredo, who has been with me since 1999, the person with whom I developed the closest relationship was the person

I spent the most time with: my driver, Angelo Spano. Angelo drove for David Peterson when he was premier from 1985 to 1990. He lived in my riding — and had more political smarts than most of my other advisers. His dedication to the job went well above the norm. He looked after me. If I was running late he'd come into the house, get the newspapers organized for me, and put the coffee on. All of these people constituted simply the best team possible.

At the end of the day, for those who keep track of these things, the public probably gives me most of the credit (or blame) for whatever transpired in the three budgets I presented to the Ontario legislature, and the ensuing changes to the province's economic circumstances. And yes, I played a key role in all of that. However, politics is like baseball. It's a team sport. You win as a team. You lose as a team. And my team came to the ballpark every day and played their hearts out. In the pages that follow I provide a more extensive roster of those who made up our teams from 1985 to 2012.

Appendix 2

LIST OF STAFF MEMBERS

Minister's Office Staff — The Peterson Years, 1985–1990

Angela Bolj	Steve Budaci	Marilyn Cap
Tony Carella	Luigi D'Ambrosio	Adriana Delfino
Karin Dillabough	John Duffy	Tracy Edstrom
Jay Fleischer	Janet Foulkes	Tony Genco
Sandy Goldman	Christine Innes	Donna Lander
Keith Mark	Penny McClure	Rose Migano
John Morrison	Liz Mulholland	Scott Nicoll
Marilyn Packer	Donna Papayanis	Andrew Pelletier
Maria Priolo	Bob Richardson	Deidre Smith
Barbara Sulzenko	Sue Wilson	Angela Zuccarelli

Minister's Office Staff — The McGuinty Years, 2003–2007

Christine Allenby	Syed Amtul	Michael Arbour
Karim Bardeesy	Laurel Currie	Cathy DiChicco
Suzana Fernandes	Diane Flanagan	Bryan Grimes
Dan Gross	Wendy Ground	Sean Hamilton
Sarah Hanafy	Susan Hanna	Jerry Khouri
Chris Kodderman	Sharon Laredo	Gina Lee

Arthur Lofsky	Daniel Malik	Charrissa McQuaig
Trina Melatti	Francine Mercier	Nicole Miller
David Morley	Sean Mullin	Herman Ng
Lori Spadorcia	Angelo Spano	Mark Stabile
Paul West	Peter Wilkinson	Paul Yeung

Queen's Park Staff

1990–1995

Adriana Delfino	Rose Mignano	Liz Mulholland
Angela Zuccarelli		

2001–2003

Steven Del Duca	Wendy Ground	Sharon Laredo
Nicole Miller		

2007–2012

Lorenzo Catuzza	Sharon Laredo	Danielle Paroyan

Constituency Office Staff

1985–1995

Anne Filetti	Sue Fiorini	Bunny Godman
Grace Isgro	Helen Poulis	Andy Sampogna
Rose Vecchiarelli		

2001–2012

Lorenzo Catuzza	Leo Di Lorenzo	Wendy Ground
Helen Poulis	Gloria Reszler	Peter Vecchiarelli
Rose Vecchiarelli	Anna Venturo	Josie Verrilli

Ontario Liberal Party Executive Council Members, 1999–2004

Sonya Catalano	David Cavaco	Jesse Davidson
Kim Donaldson	Bob Ernest	Jim Evans
Tony Genco	Helen Jennings	Tony Judd
Danielle Kotras	Marian Maloney	Laura Miller
Garry Minnie	Tim Murphy	Laura-Maria Nikolareizi
Gord Phaneuf	Delroy Prescott	Ray Rivers
Qamar Sadiq	Anne Schroder	James Scongack
Greg Sorbara	Anne Venton	Glenn Webster
Peter Wilkinson	Wright, Wilbur	

Ontario Liberal Party Executive Directors, 1999–2012

Jennifer Berney	Guy Bethell	Nicole DeKort
Jim Evans	Sarah Fink	Lindsay Hunter
Laura Miller	Dave Pryce	Simon Tunstall
Mark Tyler		

Ontario Liberal Fund Chairs, 1999–2012

Phil Olsson	Geoff Smith	Greg Sorbara

Ontario Liberal Fund Presidents, 2000–2012

Sophia Aggelonitis	Christine Hampson	Brent Johnston
Debra Roberts	Bobby Walman	Greg Wong

Ontario Liberal Party Heritage Dinner Chairs

2000 Greg Sorbara, MPP

2001 Rod Bryden

2002 James Arnett, QC

212 · GREG SORBARA

2003 Mark Cohon

2004 Michael MacMillan

2005 Larry Tanenbaum

2006 Norman Jewison

2007 Mike Lazaridis

2008 Lawrence S. Bloomberg

2009 Tony Gagliano

2010 Heather Reisman

2011 Michael Lee-Chin

2012 Helen Burstyn and Deepa Mehta

Ontario Liberal Party Campaign Director, 1999–2011
Don Guy

Local Riding Association Riding Presidents, 1985–2012

Michael Callahan	Tony Carella	Paul Castello
Steven Del Duca	Tony Genco	Renah Persofsky
Madeleine Sisti-Petruccelli	Harvey Tenenbaum	Gillian Vivona

Local Campaign Managers

1985 Nick Di Giovanni and Richard and Linda (whose last names have escaped the best efforts of our researchers)

1987 Steve Budaci

1990 Liz Mulholland and Steve Swan

2001 Steven Del Duca

2003 David Pretlove

2007 Lorenzo Catuzza

2011 Lorenzo Catuzza and Josie Verrilli

Appendix 3:

A LETTER FROM MY FATHER

S. Sorbara

1674 EGLINTON AVE. WEST
TORONTO, ONT. M6E 2H3

24 October 1985.

Dear Greg:

Thank God for modern conveniences such as the t.v. If it weren't for the t.v. and other media I would never see or hear you. I am not complaining; I know that you are a very busy man and that you are trying to do a great job.

People telephone me and ask me "Who is this guy Sorbara who is a member of the government; is he an alderman?" Some of them guess that you are my son.

I am writing this letter for the record. I believe that you will do an excellent job. I believe that you will go a long distance. But whatever distance you travel, I do hope and pray that you reach your destination by sticking to the values you were taught when you were growing up. Honesty and straightforwardness and the welfare of your fellow men must always be paramount as you strive to reach the goal you have set for yourself.

Whether or not this is your last term or whether eventually you become premier of Ontario or a member of the federal government is really not important; what is important is that when you stop travelling you can say "I did it, and I did not contaminate my mind or dirty my hands".

Love *Love Dad*

Gregory Sorbara, Esq.,
P.O. Box 73,
MAPLE, Ontario.
L0J 1E0

INDEX

minister of consumer and commercial relations, demoted to 43
minister of finance, appointed, 82
minister of finance, resigns as, 17,
114, 120
minister of labour and minister of
women's issues, appointed, 39
North York riding, wins in 1985, 30
Osgoode Hall Law School, law student at, 26
politics and political issues, interest
in, 13, 24
president of Ontario Liberal Party
by McGuinty, asked to run for, 64
public education system, 197–98
Slocan Valley, move to, 25–26
St. Michael's College School, attends, 23
Stikeman Elliott Montreal law firm,
articles at, 27, 115
University of Toronto, attends, 23
Vaughan-King-Aurora by-election,
campaign for in 2001, 68–70
Workers' Compensation Board
reform, 39
York Centre riding, wins in 1990, 47
Young Liberal expedition (1962), 24
Sorbara, Joseph, 22, 59, 114
Sorbara, Kate, 62
Greg Sorbara, begins relationship
with, 25
Greg Sorbara, meets through CYC,
24
Lynn Curtis, relationship with, 24,
25
Margo Coleman, adoption of, 25,
26
Ontario, move back to, 26
Slocan Valley, move to, 25–26
Vancouver Island, moves to, 25
Sorbara, Lucas, 25
Sorbara, Marcella, 22, 59
Sorbara, Martina, 13, 26
Sorbara, Nicholas, 13, 26, 57
Sorbara, Noelle, 26

Sorbara, Pat, 28, 49, 187, 190
Sorbara, Sam
Canada, immigration to, 20
Canadian Italian Businessmen's As-
sociation, founding father of (now
Canadian Italian Business and Pro-
fessional Association), 22
Casa d'Italia (Italian Consulate, To-
ronto), assists in repatriation of, 22
Great Depression, life during,
20–21
Guelph, Ontario, early life in, 21
insurance and real estate salesman,
22
Italian-Canadian community,
emerges as leader of, 22
land acquisition company, starts
(foundation for The Sorbara
Group), 21–22
marriage to Grace, 59
St. Michael's College (University of
Toronto), attends, 21
Sorbara Group, The, 70, 101, 109, 113–14
early establishment of, 21–22
Sousa, Charles, 171, 178, 180, 181, 183,
187, 188
Spano, Angelo, 122, 208, 209
"Spills Bill," 35
St. Basil's Church, 33
Stabile, Mark, 206–07, 210
Starr, Patti, 42, 49, 50
STORM (Save the Oak Ridges Moraine)
coalition, 69
Sullivan, Father Basil Francis, 21
Sulzenko, Barbara, 35, 50, 202, 209

Takhar, Harinder, 71, 85–86, 171, 177,
180, 181, 183
Thatcher, Margaret, 17–18
Thomson, Sarah, 134–35, 140
Tilson, David, 75
Toronto Blue Jays Fantasy Camp, 67
Toronto Star, 53, 68, 126, 133
Toronto Transit Commission (TTC), 85,
98, 100

Available at your favourite bookseller

 DUNDURN

Visit us at
Dundurn.com | @dundurnpress | Facebook.com/dundurnpress
Pinterest.com/dundurnpress